THE BOOKSELLER
AT THE END
OF THE WORLD

THE BOOKSELLER
AT THE END
OF THE WORLD

RUTH SHAW

ALLEN&UNWIN
SYDNEY • MELBOURNE • AUCKLAND • LONDON

First published in 2022

Text © Ruth Shaw, 2022

The photographs in the picture section are from the author's private collection.

Extract on page 175 from 'Do not go gentle into that good night' by Dylan Thomas © The Dylan Thomas Trust. Reproduced with kind permission of David Higham Associates.

Allen & Unwin
Level 2, 10 College Hill, Freemans Bay
Auckland 1011, New Zealand
Phone: (64 9) 377 3800
Email: auckland@allenandunwin.com
Web: www.allenandunwin.co.nz

83 Alexander Street
Crows Nest NSW 2065, Australia
Phone: (61 2) 8425 0100

A catalogue record for this book is available from the National Library of New Zealand.

ISBN 978 1 98854 775 6

Design by Saskia Nicol
Set in Feijoa
Printed in China by Hang Tai Printing Company Limited

10 9 8 7 6 5

For my amazing mother, Freda (November 1925 – June 1972), and for my incredible husband, Lance: my first and last love.

CONTENTS

CHAPTER 1
TWO WEE BOOKSHOPS
11

CHAPTER 2
THE START OF BOOKS AND BUSINESS
19

CHAPTER 3
KNOW WHEN TO HOLD 'EM
31

CHAPTER 4
NASEBY
37

CHAPTER 5
1963
45

CHAPTER 6
OFF TO THE NAVY
56

CHAPTER 7
STEWART ISLAND AND MEETING LANCE
66

CHAPTER 8
WORKING FOR THE ARCHBISHOP
77

CHAPTER 9
ALL ABOARD
84

CHAPTER 10
MY BRIEF CAREER AS A BURGLAR
96

CHAPTER 11
TRAGEDY RETURNS
112

CHAPTER 12
ARRIVING IN RABAUL
118

CHAPTER 13
PLEASE WORRY
127

CHAPTER 14
LETTERS FROM HOME
144

CHAPTER 15
SLIPPING AWAY
154

CHAPTER 16
DO NOT GO GENTLE
165

CHAPTER 17
THE MADHATTER'S MANSION
179

CHAPTER 18
MARRIAGE, MARIJUANA AND THE MENAGERIE
194

CHAPTER 19
A KIND OF MAGIC
208

CHAPTER 20
RESIST MUCH, OBEY LITTLE . . .
221

CHAPTER 21
FIGHTING FOR THE OPPOSITION
230

CHAPTER 22
HOME BECKONS
243

CHAPTER 23
ARRIVING HOME
253

CHAPTER 24
THE ADVENTURES OF LANCE
266

CHAPTER 25
FINDING MY SON
281

CHAPTER 26
MY BLUE-EYED BOY
292

CHAPTER 27
THE BOOKSELLER AT THE END OF THE WORLD
299

CHAPTER 28
HOME STREET
311

ACKNOWLEDGEMENTS
318

ABOUT THE AUTHOR
320

CHAPTER 1

TWO WEE BOOKSHOPS

On the corner of Hillside Road and Home Street, opposite Lake Manapōuri, sit Two Wee Bookshops, painted in a medley of bright colours and surrounded by plants, curiosities and the odd bookshop pet or two.

Each morning from late September through to mid-April, weekends included, I open my Two Wee Bookshops. My green 1961 Fiat 500 is prominently parked on the corner of Hillside Road and the Southern Scenic Highway, advertising 'the Smallest Bookshop in New Zealand'. I put out the OPEN sign on the corner of Home Street and then start setting up the various tables and brightly painted old school desks with a variety of books. On the blackboard I write: OPEN, PLEASE RING BELL LOUDLY IF I AM NOT HERE. A ship's bell hangs beside the door and I can hear it ringing from nearly anywhere on our large, tree-covered property.

I was 70 when I decided to open these bookshops, as a fun retirement 'hobby'. I had opened my first bookshop almost 30 years earlier, as part of a yacht charter operation that my husband Lance and I ran called Fiordland Ecology Holidays.

Bookshops in general attract people who love books, but my Two Wee Bookshops are a beacon to everyone who travels past. It might be the bright colours, or the old windows and door, or the fact that they really are so small. Tibor, from Budapest, was driving past the small cottages when he caught a glimpse of the word 'Bookshop' on my corner sign, did a quick U-turn and ended up living in our garden hut for a month. He was a male nurse on an extended holiday, living in his old station wagon. In return for food and accommodation, he worked in the small forest that surrounds our home. He loved books and spent a lot of his time sitting in the bookshop, reading and chatting to my customers. When I had to be away, he opened the bookshop for me and successfully sold lots of books. When he left, there were a lot of tears; he didn't want to go and we were sad to say goodbye.

And then we met Jana, the young German girl who came into the bookshop, sat on a chair and started to cry, blowing her nose into a well-soaked tissue. I hugged her, holding her close to me as she wept. Her relationship had just ended, she told me. I took her inside and Lance took over in the shop, in his usual understanding and compassionate way. He is the bookshop's personal counsellor and serves endless cups of tea and coffee throughout the day. Lance is also my handyman, my 'Quick, help me!' man, and he joins me in setting up the bookshops every morning. Jana stayed with us for a week.

Along came Lily from Poland, who was so homesick she just wanted to talk — and wow, did she talk! I heard about her entire family, right down to her grandparents; where she went to school and where she had travelled in New Zealand. At the end of this breathless and mostly one-sided conversation, she told me about the breakup of her relationship.

Adam from Australia arrived. He looked about 21, a broad fellow with a cheeky smile. He was working in Milford Sound and had a few days off.

'Just want to know how to read a book,' he said.

I had never heard this before, but thought if anyone should know how to read a book, it would be a book dealer.

'What are you interested in, Adam?' I asked.

'Not much. I do like growing and smoking dope.'

I was a little taken aback at his openness — he didn't know me. Then I considered my appearance from a stranger's point of view. I was dressed in my trademark baggy Indian cotton pants, with a tunic down to my knees, topped off with a colourful hat. I could see his point. 'I have just the book for you,' I said. 'Just wait — it's in my own library and it's not actually for sale.'

Bogor, written by Burton Silver and published in 1980, is a book of cartoon strips about a lone woodsman named Bogor who befriends a hedgehog who grows dope. The hedgehog's diet consists of snails that are farmed and fed on his marijuana plants. The strip featured in the *New Zealand Listener* magazine from 1973 until 1995, becoming New Zealand's longest-running published cartoon series. We all fell in love with *Bogor*, which was pretty radical for the time. *Bogor* books soon appeared and are now collectable.

I returned to the shop with the book and told Adam the story behind Bogor and the friendly hedgehog who ate stoned snails. 'You'll love this. It's easy to read and I'm sure once you start, you won't stop!'

Adam did start reading. When he returned the book, he said he'd been on Trade Me, hoping to buy some to start his own collection.

———

ONE DAY A man named Alan arrived. He sat on the doorstep in silence, his shoulders stooped, his head nearly touching his knees.

'Why don't you come in and sit down?' I said to him. 'I'll lock the door so you can have some time to yourself.'

'No, I wouldn't expect you to do that,' he said, but he did stand up and come into the shop. I raced out, turned the OPEN sign around, cleaned the blackboard and closed the door. We just sat quietly for a few minutes until eventually I introduced myself. I looked across at him and he was crying.

Our home is right next door to the bookshops, so I ran in and asked Lance to make two cups of coffee and bring them to the shop. This is a frequent request during my busy times when people are waiting to get into the already crowded bookshop; more than five customers and there is no room to move! Lance entertains people who are waiting with amazing stories of his life, and makes tea and coffee. Thankfully he is a reader too, so he is happy to discuss books if required.

Coffee was duly delivered: one with milk only, the other with milk and sugar. Lance had guessed correctly — Alan was a milk and sugar man.

'Thanks, Ruth,' Alan said. 'I think I was meant to come here — except I don't actually read books.'

'Lots of people come here who don't read books.'

'It was the colours and the bell hanging by the door that attracted me. I am a fireman from New South Wales, and I was ordered to take some leave. So here I am.' He sighed and looked up at me. 'Do you think I have let my workmates down? Because I do. They're still out there. And no matter where I go, I still smell smoke.' The Australian bush fires that year were so horrendous that even here in Manapōuri, at the bottom of the South Island of New Zealand, we could smell the smoke and our skies bled with the colour of fire.

We talked for over an hour. The horrors of what he had been through, and had to go back to, made me want to cry.

Eventually he stood up, put his cup on the small desk, pulled a tissue from the box I have ready for all occasions, and blew his nose. 'Thanks, Ruth. You were exactly what a worn-out old fireman needed!'

I hugged him, looking up at him as he was so much taller than me, and smiled. I knew he was off to walk the Kepler Track the next day. 'Try and smell the forest,' I said. 'Breathe the mountain air and know that when you go back, you'll be ready to work alongside your mates again. I have a wee book for you.' I handed him a copy of *Furry Logic: A guide to life's little challenges*. 'This will make you smile — and possibly even laugh.'

Alan grinned. I opened the door and, as he walked around the corner towards the lake, I turned the sign around to OPEN.

Some days I give away more books than I sell, which is one of the delights of being retired and not having the pressure to make money. The joy of giving away the perfect book is far more rewarding than making a sale.

——

THE SMALLER BOOKSHOP, which is for children, is tucked in behind a fence with only the front showing; the red door is just over a metre in height.

Children come and go from the Children's Bookshop; often they sit and read while they cuddle one of the soft toys sitting in a row on the bottom shelves, awaiting precious attention. The mothers, fathers and grandparents find a book from their childhood and as they read, they drift away into their memories.

In one corner I have a lending library. In the days before Covid-19 I let children take a book home for the night, together with a soft toy, each one named by the first child to borrow it. When the toys are returned I wash them and hang them out to dry. Often my clothesline is full of furry animals hanging by their ears or tails. Some of their names are Honey and Maple, the twin bears; Blizzard MacMurray, the very white furry cat; Mornington the cat; Camo the camel; Moon the yellow duck and Bouncy the rabbit.

Eep the little white lamb had been on a sleepover for two nights, and came back slightly damp and covered in mud and grass.

'Wow! Looks like Eep had a great holiday,' I said.

'I put her in the paddock with the sheep at night so she wouldn't be lonely.'

'Great idea. I'm sure she loved it.'

Eep is now back on the shelf looking very white after her bath.

Tama, who spends his holidays in Manapōuri with his grandparents, frequently drops into the bookshop. He is very serious, extremely thoughtful and often quite funny. He took Growl, the small stuffed lion, home for a sleepover. Before he left the shop I explained to him that I had put Growl through the washing machine and his roar was no longer a roar, but more like the sound of someone slowly drowning.

Tama smiled and said, 'That's okay.'

When he returned Growl the next day he looked me in the eye, and said, 'I think you were too hard on Growl. His roar isn't that bad!'

One of the favourite books from the lending library is *The Velveteen Rabbit*, written by Margery Williams in 1922. Rabbit asks his friend the Skin Horse, 'What is real?'

'Real isn't how you are made,' the Skin Horse replies. 'It's a thing that happens to you. When a child loves you for a long, long time, not just to play with, but REALLY loves you, then you become Real.'

I have read this book many times and this one sentence reminds me of the times in my life when I really came to understand the meaning of the word *real*.

CHAPTER 2

THE START OF BOOKS AND BUSINESS

My father worked as a fireman on the railways from 1941 to 1946, the year I was born. He told us many stories of his time with the railways: Engine K942 was his favourite. New Zealand Rail introduced this engine because it was able to handle our mountainous terrain and could carry more heavy freight. I think I inherited my father's love of trains: throughout my life, if I was not sailing on a boat, I was on a train.

Mum was 19 when she married Dad, who was 21. It was 1944. They moved in with Dad's parents, Gran and Pop, for the first three years of their marriage; my sister Jill and I were both born while we were living with them.

Gran and Pop's home overlooked the Avon River in Christchurch — a perfect family home with five bedrooms, a large kitchen, dining room, lounge and even a laundry with a boiler. Jill and I shared a room with Aunty Maureen, the twin of Aunty Lorraine, who were only ten years older than us and the youngest of Gran's five children. Aunty Joan, the eldest, was already married and living up in the North Island. Numerous foster children also lived with us — we called them uncles and aunties.

Gran ran the huge household with a strong but gentle hand. Pop was always out in his shed working on bikes, or over in his brother Jim's famous shop, Hobdays Cycles, which he opened in 1943 on Colombo Street. It is still trading today.

A buxom woman, Gran wore an apron every day, her hair always up in a tight bun. She was nearly always smiling and full of hugs and cuddles. I loved her immensely. It was Gran who said many times, as she hugged and kissed me on the head, 'Ruthie, I know you try to be good, but you just aren't.'

She made us pants out of flour-bag material, and we had Sad Cake on Sundays. Suet replaced the butter, making the cake heavy, so it often arrived at the table with a sunken centre. As a treat we would have jam and cream on buttered bread.

Mum and Dad's first home of their own was in Bangor Street, a block back from the Avon River and a short walk to Gran's. We moved there in 1949. It was a very small wooden bungalow, always in a state of being rebuilt by Dad. This kept him extremely busy but Uncle Ivan and Dad decided to take on another venture: breeding chickens on an industrial scale for meat. They found a piece of land suitable to house and raise the 100-plus hens, but at the last minute, after the birds had been bought and paid for, the landowner pulled out of the deal. Consequently, the free-range frozen-chicken enterprise was sited in our small back yard.

When the chickens arrived, Dad had already pulled down the entire back wall of our house, exposing both the kitchen and our small bedroom to the back yard. He had enclosed it with hessian bags, which were supposed to keep out the cold. Frequently we would wake up to hear chickens quietly clucking to themselves as they snuck in under the hessian sacking to roost along our bedheads or in some other cosy place for the night.

The chicken venture came to an abrupt halt when the neighbours complained, but only after the chickens had taken complete control of our back yard and home.

Dad was always coming up with new ideas, which frequently involved the whole family. (This trait has definitely been handed down to me!) When we moved from Bangor Street to Oxford Terrace, Dad immediately decided to turn the big home into a boarding house.

Two of our first boarders were Bill and Maurice, the

first two male nurses at Christchurch Public Hospital. Maurice later became the matron at Silverstream Hospital in Upper Hutt. There were always dramas going on as they were openly gay and a couple, which was a big deal in the 1950s. Bill became Uncle Bill to us. Mum ran the boarding house while Dad was away over the summer months goldmining down at the Deep Lead mine at Matakanui in Central Otago.

Once Dad had finished rebuilding, repairing and painting, the Oxford Terrace house was sold and we moved to Conference Street in 1953.

In the early 1940s Grandad Benn, my mother's father, bought a two-room bach at Pile Bay, a tiny secluded beach tucked under high, tussock-covered hills on Banks Peninsula, within rowing distance of Rīpapa Island. He had also acquired a clinker-built lifeboat with massive oars, which we learnt to row. All of our summer holidays were spent at Pile Bay with our cousins, Ken and David. We ran barefoot and wild over the hills and around the rocky shoreline; we learnt to row and fish, and dig for cockles and pipis; we grass-sledged down the tussock hills; and at night we would sit on a hilltop and watch the interisland ferry leave Lyttelton Harbour on its overnight trip to Wellington.

When Dad and Uncle Ivan came across for weekends we kids would sleep head to toe in the bunks, leaving four bunks for our parents. Uncle Ivan was married to

Mum's sister Philliss (known as Aunty Fan). At night, the kerosene Tilley lamps cast shadows across the room with a continuous gentle sigh. How I loved the smell of the musky bunkroom, always salty with a hint of warm kerosene. Under my mattress I had piles of books that I faithfully read every holiday, often by candlelight.

We played cards, did puzzles, washed outside standing in a big enamel basin, cleaned our teeth in the sea, and wore the same clothes every day. Grandad made fishing nets out of cotton twine; when he finished a net he soaked it in cold tea so it wouldn't rot.

Rīpapa Island, also known as Fort Jervois, was a child's dream playground, the seeding of incredible memories that I still carry. It has quite a history, having been the site of a Ngāi Tahu pā, then a quarantine station for new immigrants in the late 1880s, a prison for 150 followers of Te Whiti, and then a coastal defence base during both world wars.

The fortification has high architectural and aesthetic significance and now has a Category 1 listing with Heritage New Zealand as a rare example of an 1880s underground fort. It has four disappearing gun pits connected by tunnels to underground magazines and living quarters. The main entrance was given a castle-like appearance, with a stone wall, battlements and mock cross arrow slits.

The small island is surrounded by rocks, and a masonry sea wall was built around the fort. The only way to get onto the island was over a swingbridge or up the boat ramp. Off the main courtyard we used to enter the underground fort, a mysterious maze of small tunnels mostly closed off with iron gates. It was frightening but also absolutely thrilling. In the cool darkness we explored the embankments where huge guns remained in place, and cell doors still opened and closed.

Our family still has the bach at Pile Bay. It now has solar panels, a composting toilet, two bedrooms and a shower. The old kerosene fridge has been replaced by a solar-powered one, and the wonderful old yellow and green coal range has given way to a gas cooker. We were the grandchildren back then; now we are the grandparents, the carriers of the stories.

———

DAD WAS ON the move again: Conference Street was up for sale. We shifted to Fitzgerald Avenue into a large two-storey house in which a grocery store occupied most of the ground floor. At the age of eight I had my first paid job: helping Mum and Dad in the shop. Jill, aged ten, earned £2 a week for writing names on newspapers, packing up orders and working late in the shop once a week to help Mum lock up.

Dad explained to me that the minimum wage for women was just over three shillings an hour; as I was only eight, he would pay me 1/6 an hour. After school I was responsible for weighing and packaging rice, flour and sugar, which arrived in large sacks, and loose tea out of large wooden boxes. Dad encouraged me to learn about profit and loss, how to budget, and the importance of saving. I tucked my wages into a jar at the bottom of my wardrobe; like my father, I already had plans for how to increase my weekly income.

My first solo business venture was breeding and selling pet mice, fully supported by my father. He made me two- and three-storey mouse houses out of wooden fruit boxes from the shop, and Mum taught me how to look after them. I was determined to make a success of the mouse business: failure was not an option. As soon as the wee mice were old enough, I piled them into a travel box, which fitted onto my bike carrier, and took them to school to sell. I sold them in paper bags lined with straw for sixpence each, sex guaranteed.

My business was going well until the nuns decided that the school grounds were not a suitable place for trading mice. Even though all of the remaining mice were sold off very cheaply, I had made a profit. I bought my parents a parakeet, which Dad named Floyd. We later found out that he was a she when she laid an egg on his shoulder. Dad loved her. Mum tolerated her.

———

CENTRAL OTAGO IS steeped in the history of goldmining, from the coast of Dunedin inland to Palmerston, over the well-known Pigroot into the Maniototo Plain and then down into the Ōmakau, Clyde and Alexandra area. I had heard older relatives talk about gold fever but never gave it much thought until I witnessed the frenzied state my father got into when he started to work his own claim in Matakanui, which used to be called Tinkers.

Dad had become the sole stakeholder of the Deep Lead mine after the older partners died. To comply with the law the mine had to be worked every year; if it wasn't, the land could be re-staked by anyone and Dad would lose his rights. The problem was that the main vein of gold was under a small lake, so the mine could only be worked after the winter ice had thawed and the lake level was lower. The alluvial gold was mainly extracted through a water-driven sluice.

Over the summer holidays, Mum and Dad employed a manager for the shop and we all went down to the mine at the base of the Dunstan Range. The summers were extremely hot, which suited my dark complexion, but both Mum and Jill suffered from sunburn as they were so fair. Mum was only 153 cm (5 foot) tall but there was no end to what she achieved at the mine. Dad worked from daylight until dark on the sluice, Mum shovelled the resulting paydirt, Jill rocked the cradle, and I washed the mats and panned with a small gold pan Dad bought me. Dad would yell out encouragement: 'Keep up the good work, no need to slow down. The day has just started so we have a long day ahead of us.'

After a full day of work Dad would collect the paydirt, dry it in front of a fire, then place it on newspaper that was shaped into a 'V'. He would gently shake the newspaper while quietly blowing the dry, payable dirt. With experience and patience, he would see the gold dust and flakes lying across the top of the paper, separated from the dirt.

At the end of each week we would go over to the hut of Old Sandy Anderton, a hardy goldminer, who would prepare the collected gold dust to sell at the bank in Ōmakau. He would cut a deep hole in a big potato, pour in the gold dust and then block the hole with the extracted potato 'plug'. The potato was then placed among hot coals in the fire for the night. The next morning a small gold nugget was nestled inside the cooked potato. An ounce of gold sold for £12.

TALES FROM THE BOOKSHOPS: 'TELL YOUR STORIES'

I HAD BEEN asked to speak to the local Women's Fellowship Group. Diane MacDonald, the president of the group, had heard me on Kim Hill's *Saturday Morning* radio show on RNZ and asked me to come along. 'Just talk about your bookshops and . . . oh! Of course, more about your life.'

As I pulled in to the Salvation Army carpark, Diane came across to meet me.

'Terrible morning,' she said. 'I'm so sorry — it's been chaotic. One of our dear ladies suddenly died last night and I have yet to tell everyone.'

My mind went into overdrive: how do you address a group of women who have just received the news that their friend has died? I had planned to tell stories that would make them laugh, but how could I do that in such an extremely distressing situation?

Diane stood at the lectern and delivered the awful news, then added that we *must* carry on and enjoy the morning together. She introduced me.

I expressed my condolences and spoke about how often we are taken by surprise when someone dies. I have always believed that everyone has a story to tell, so I stressed how important it was for their families to hear their stories, and even record them.

'You don't have to have an exciting or drama-filled life to have a story. It's just as important to tell your children and grandchildren about growing up on a farm, walking to school in all weathers, sometimes in bare feet; to recall how your mother had home remedies for coughs, headaches and insect bites. Who made your first dance dress? My grandmother made our pants out of flour bags! Do you remember how cakes were made out of lard or fat? Your telephone was on a "party line", and you knew the local gossip would be listening in. Remember how important and exciting it was to receive a letter?'

By this time I was nearly in tears, as I recounted stories my two grandmothers had told me.

'Write your stories,' I said to them. 'Please write your stories.'

Thankfully I was able to climb over the sense of sadness and managed to entertain these amazing women. We all ended up laughing — the morning was precious and memorable.

After my session, while I was eating my way through an embarrassing pile of wonderful food, Diane asked if she could organise to bring the Winton Book Club up to Manapōuri to hold a meeting at my bookshops. I said I thought it was a wonderful idea.

A few months later they arrived in three cars, laden down

with supplies for an incredible finger-food lunch. It was a fabulous day, sitting out in the sunshine, all with sunhats on, chatting and laughing as we ate our way through the delicious lunch. As they discussed their latest book club choice, it was obvious that some had enjoyed it and others hadn't, so this made for lively debate.

As I was halfway through writing this book at the time, I listened intently and wondered how an open discussion of my completed book would play out. Sex, drugs, foul language, a couple of arrests and multiple marriages were bound to generate lively debate, I decided!

CHAPTER 3

KNOW WHEN TO HOLD 'EM

It was 1953 and I was seven years old. We had just moved to a two-storey house with the very posh name of Brixton House, located in Conference Street, Christchurch. This was the third house we had lived in over the past six years since initially living with Gran and Pop for a year after I was born. Buying old houses, doing them up and selling them on was only one of numerous careers my father embarked on during his life.

This one was an older-style home with no front garden, as the front door was only a few feet back from the footpath. A huge walnut tree shadowed the back yard and in the far corner was a vegetable garden.

Opposite the kitchen door at the back of the house was a small bedroom where Nanny, my mother's mother, slept. Nanny, Ellen Martha Daisy, had been living with us since she had left Grandad, Ethelbert Ponsonby Benn — I have always loved his name. He moved in with our aunty.

Nanny was always getting visitors but we were only allowed into her room when we were invited. She was a tall, stern-looking woman with a pinched mouth and dark, near-black eyes that were alert and often sad. Short, dark grey, crimped hair capped her head, glasses with pale rims sat high on her nose, and she always wore buttoned-up dresses. Her most beautiful feature I recall was her hands. Long elegant fingers, pale and straight, and carefully shaped nails with wee moons peeping over the quick. She loved to play cards; in fact she was a gambler of rather grand proportions, gambling away the family inheritance.

It wasn't until years later when Jill and I talked about Nanny that I recognised how astute she had been. She was tender with Jill, reading her stories while tucked up in bed together; there was never a cross word. Jill had long blonde plaits, blue eyes and she was always well behaved. As for me, I was untidy, a tomboy with short black hair, always full of questions and frequently in trouble. I never experienced tenderness from Nanny — hardly even a thank you when I changed the dressings on her ulcerated legs from the age of nine.

I didn't love Nanny as I loved Gran, but she taught me

some of the life skills I needed to navigate my chaotic life. From an exceedingly early age, I learnt from Nanny how to play cribbage, pontoon and show poker, as well as the basics of a few card tricks. She taught me how to hold the cards correctly in my small hands, how to shuffle without showing anyone the card on the bottom of the deck, and to quickly play a card with confidence and a fixed facial expression, giving nothing away. Although my hands were so much smaller than hers I held my cards as elegantly as Nanny did, holding them close so 'no one could cheat'.

These skills ended up being lifelong lessons. Whenever I was short on money, I played cards to win. Most important were the key tricks of how to bluff and manipulate. 'If you have a bad hand, it's no use looking like you have a bad hand,' Nanny would tell me. She taught me how to look convincing and to hold eye contact even when you have a crap hand.

This wasn't just for card-playing; all through my life the things Nanny taught me came in handy, over and over again. If I was in a situation I didn't want to be in, I needed to have the confidence to show the world I was holding a winning hand.

When I was a bit older, about ten, I would go down to the pub with my father and Uncle Ivan and we would play euchre and 500. I was the only young girl in the room. I used to partner Dad, and we played very well together. I remember Dad saying to me, many years later when I was leaving to go join the navy, that life was like playing cards. You're given a hand, and the way you play that hand may determine the rest of the month, the rest of the year, or the rest of your life. But you don't have time to plan, because if you hesitate when you're playing cards, people may guess your next move. His lasting piece of advice was: 'Whenever you're in a situation, just think of your life as a pack of cards and imagine how you would play that hand. You can turn a losing hand into a winning hand by the card you play next.'

Throughout my whole life I have loved playing cards. Thankfully I never fell victim to gambling, but twice in my life card-playing was to lead to a very interesting situation — the two occasions vastly different. One played out in Papeete, French Polynesia, when I was sailing around the Pacific on the *Cutty Sark*, and the other in Rabaul, Papua New Guinea, where I worked for just on four years.

TALES FROM THE
BOOKSHOPS:
AN UNLIKELY PILGRIM

—

A BIG MAN arrived at the bookshop door. He was dressed in well-worn tramping clothes, his slight body odour informing me that he was just off the mountains. He sat on the step and took off his wet, muddy boots, placing them on the doormat.

'Just off a track?' I asked, even though it was obvious.

'Ten days, a bit of bush bashing. Hope you don't mind.'

I laughed. 'You look like you need a cup of strong coffee. Milk and sugar?'

'That would be ace, thanks. Two big sugars.'

When I returned to the shop with two cups of coffee he was sitting on the floor, searching through an opened map of Fiordland. 'This place is incredible, isn't it? You can chase the sun every day and still there are more mountains it can hide behind.'

'Planning on going back then?' I asked.

He nodded.

'Walking away from something or walking towards something?' I ventured.

He looked up at me from the floor, where he sat drinking his coffee. 'Just walking. Soaking it all up, building the soul.' He had a wonderful way with words.

He told me he was 'lost at the present time', and liked being by himself so he could sort it out.

'Staying at the camping ground for a few days, then I'll head off again. Mind if I drop in and out? I like books but my pack isn't big enough to carry them.'

'Come by any time,' I told him. 'If I'm closed, come and knock on our front door and I'll give you the key.'

Over the next three days Hamish came and went. He had shaved, his clothes had been washed, but he was still wearing his old boots.

Soon I knew enough about him to give him a book I knew he would really love, a book he would never have thought to pick up and read.

'Hamish, I'm going to give you a book and you *have* to squeeze it into your pack.'

He took the book and smiled at the title: *The Unlikely Pilgrimage of Harold Fry* by Rachel Joyce.

'I think Harold's shoes are a little like your boots,' I said. 'When you've finished it, leave it in a hut for someone else to read.'

'No Ruth, I won't do that,' he said. 'This is my book — you've chosen it for me. I'm not leaving it anywhere.'

He went to shake my hand, but instead I reached up and hugged him.

'Stay safe, Hamish.'

CHAPTER 4

NASEBY

In 1957 we moved to the little town of Naseby in Central Otago, recognised as one of the smallest and oldest boroughs in New Zealand, with a population of just over 100. It still had a mayor and city councillors. Much to Dad's delight, we were in the heart of goldmining country.

It was in May 1863 when gold was first found in a gully near Mt Ida, close to Naseby's present location. Over the next few months a canvas town grew as miners left the Dunstan goldfields to tramp through the winter snow up to the new find, 2000 feet above sea level. In a very short period of time the population of the canvas town doubled when payable dirt was found in the Hogburn Stream, which flows through Naseby. The town was officially called Naseby in 1873.

Our house was divided in two: half was a butcher shop with a boiler room, and we lived in the other half. For Mum, the move had meant leaving her sister and family in Christchurch so she felt quite isolated. My sister Jill hated Naseby, as she had thrived in the formal structure of our Catholic girls' college, where she was taught by the Sisters of Mercy, and now had to continue her education at Ranfurly High, a small-town co-ed school. But I loved our new home. I think Dad, Beswick (our Persian cat) and I blossomed in Naseby, whereas Jill and Mum 'made the most of the move'.

Naseby Primary School, where I went, had only two rooms, both with potbelly stoves to keep us warm in the winter. We didn't start each day on our knees reciting the rosary, we didn't have to learn Latin, or endlessly sing hymns, we didn't have to attend Mass numerous times each week or read the catechism. I didn't work after school, only over school holidays, so I had time to play and explore, and sport became an important part of my life.

The little Athenaeum reading room was only two doors down from our house. It was dark inside; a solitary light draped feelings of mystery, adventure and intrigue throughout. Many of the books were extremely old, with leather or cloth boards, the gilt titles faded, tissue-paper-thin pages that crinkled when turned. For me it was delicious; I remember sitting at the small wooden table and just hugging a big book because I loved it so much.

Dad became the town clerk, while also trading as the local butcher. He kept the rates book under the counter in the butcher shop and people came to the shop to pay. He was also the ice curling master, responsible for preparing the ice for the bonspiels, or tournaments, and of course he was goldmining on the side.

William (Billy) Strong was the watchmaker in Naseby; he lived in a tiny cob cottage in Derwent Street, just across the road from the post office. His father had opened the small, cluttered watchmaker's shop in 1868, in Leven Street. There it still stood, the walls covered with every imaginable type of clock, not a single one showing the correct time.

Billy would occasionally open the shop to the public, so they could gaze upon the beautiful fob watches, wristwatches and clocks. Behind the wooden counter were boxes of watches that he worked on at his own leisurely pace, poking around in dark corners for some nearly forgotten piece. It was Billy who told me all about fob watches, explaining the importance of the length and weight of the chain, the spring, the gears and the tiny wheels. He continued in the business until 1967.

When autumn was at its height, the yellowed needles of the larch trees gathered in the streets, and the first fall of snow would cover the hills. This was the time of year when the gravedigger pre-dug a few graves up at the cemetery, as once the harsh winter came, the ground was frozen.

'Chrome Dome' was the nickname for the gravedigger — a tall, well-built, bald man in his forties. With a ready smile, he would salute the old men gathered in the street as he walked past. 'How's the lads today, then?' he asked nearly every morning. He had registered with Dad, as town clerk, to dig four new holes to get through the winter.

'Glad you're all looking so well going into winter,' he said to the old men, perhaps thinking of his winter numbers, and strode off with his shovel over his shoulder.

Frequently, when a new hole was dug, an old grave was exposed — the early records were not particularly accurate. Established in 1860, the Naseby cemetery is one of the oldest in New Zealand. The Chinese goldminers' graves were tucked under the huge trees near the fenceline, their names engraved in Chinese on flat slabs. Many of the early graves were pauper graves.

Winter presented itself early in Central; the mountains stood calmly as the first dusting of snow cloaked their tops and sought to fill the valleys. Then clouds would sneak softly across the sky, steadily covering the lower hills, engulfing everything that stood in their way. The air would quickly turn bitingly cold. Naseby was ready to hunker down.

The stillness was so complete that first winter that I sat curled up, eyes wide in wonder as I watched the glowing fires of gaping pinecones, gathered in autumn, burn steadily, sending swirling columns of smoke upward, spreading their scent through the air.

Through my bedroom window I watched my first snowfall, entranced. The first snowflake fell like a cotton-wool ball, drifting insanely, a tiny parachute dancing. It was as though this little flake had been sent to announce the grand opening of the most spectacular ballet, played only once a year but lasting for months. Now tiny ballerinas descended in their hundreds, thousands, millions, all dressed in white, dancing faster and faster.

Pretty soon I couldn't see the stone bridge across the dirt road. I quickly dressed and ran to the recreation ground, my boots crunching in the deep snow. I was bundled up in winter layers, with only my eyes peeping through various scarves that wrapped around my face. The fenceposts had donned their winter tam-o'-shanters, white and crisp, some even sporting pine needles at jaunty angles. Heavy braids of snow started to weigh down the telegraph wires.

—

THIS IS WHERE my story really begins, in the heart of the Maniototo Plain.

'Cold enough to freeze the cockles off your bum,' my father said as we approached the ambling figure of the mysterious watchmaker, Billy Strong. 'Better light your pipe and give it a few blows to warm your nose — seems to be growing an icicle.' The still erect but ageing figure of Billy came closer, to within hearing distance.

'I'd better light my pipe. Knew it was going to snow — the trees, you know. And the birds.' With a huge, well-used handkerchief he wiped his equally large, hooked nose, withdrew his fob watch, checked the time and nodded. 'As I was saying, been here too many years not to know when it's going to snow. A good fall today; even the plains will have a dusting.'

'Yes, I'd say so,' replied Dad, standing with his feet apart, hands in pockets, his tobacco pouch poking out of his jersey pocket and his butcher's apron tied securely around his slightly round tummy. His blue eyes were surrounded by laugh lines; his blond hair, slightly receding, was capped with his cheese-cutter. 'Keeps the ears warm,' he would say, inexplicably since his cap didn't even cover them. And there, beneath his grand family nose, emerged his glowing pipe, black with age and beautifully seasoned.

'Going over to join the boys, then?' he called to Billy, nodding towards the grocery shop and its well-used long bench, seemingly a part of the window display. That was where the group of old men, including Billy, gathered each morning, across the road from Dad's butcher shop. They had all arrived in Naseby as young men, eager to work, go goldmining, marry and settle down. Now, in their later years, they spent their mornings sitting in the sun, smoking their pipes, reminiscing and occasionally dozing.

Already the bench was half-full of decrepit 'boys', just sitting, their pipes smoking away cheerily under their constantly dripping noses. As each new one joined them they would doff their hats, mumble something about the weather, and then resume their slumped positions. There would be much nodding, mumbling and smoke puffing. By mid-morning the bench would be full, the old wheezing engines of the goldrush days reporting for their daily tuning.

—

AFTER NASEBY PRIMARY School, I joined Jill on the school bus to Ranfurly High. Our English teacher, Miss Alexandra, said I had excellent writing ability and encouraged me to read and write. Our maths teacher, Mr Hill, on the other hand, eventually stopped asking me questions and just left me to daydream (and write).

Geography introduced me to maps. I studied their detail — longitude, latitude, topography — and lost myself in thoughts about the oceans and the equator. I researched different countries, learnt about the animals and people, and strongly debated against the concept of the British Commonwealth.

Books on the Second World War were now appearing

in the school library, including *The Diary of Anne Frank*, which I read at the age of thirteen. Anne wrote her diary at the same age and died only two years later, which made a huge impression on me. I had no intention of staying at school any longer than I needed to; life for me was not to be found in a classroom.

In the first week of 1963, Naseby held a centennial celebration, the whole town dressed up in period costume. There was a parade down the main street, a beard-growing competition, sausages on bread, athletics in the recreation grounds, gold-panning demonstrations and dancing at night. They even screened a film in the town hall. Ross McMillan, later known as 'Blue Jeans, the poet from Naseby', raced around the town on his horse; for our amusement he jumped over a vehicle. A local man lay looking very dead in the old hearse as it was pulled down the main street by two horses.

The parade ended at the Royal Hotel, with everyone crushing in. When it was full, the remainder filled up the Ancient Briton Hotel. The drinking, singing and eating began, with everyone forgetting about the poor man in the hearse, who by then was hammering on the glass wanting to get out. Eventually someone noticed, but it took a while to free him as the door on the hearse had jammed shut and they didn't want to break the glass.

I remember 1963 for two reasons, one being the centennial, and the other being that it was the year I was raped.

CHAPTER 5

1963

During my teenage years a dance was held once a month in one of the community halls around the Maniototo. Large crowds usually attended, from early teens through to their grandparents. We danced the Gay Gordons, the Highland Rambler, the foxtrot and waltz, all of which we were taught at high school. When we first learnt the waltz we were paired up with another girl, counting 'one, two, three, one, two, three' and trying not to giggle. Not until we could waltz and foxtrot around the school hall with straight backs, our heads held high and arms perfectly positioned, were we permitted to dance with a boy. Suddenly we felt grown up, promoted into the world of adulthood, even though we were only fifteen or sixteen.

By that stage I smoked Matinée cigarettes, I played a serious game of hockey with girls up to six years older than me, I could play a good round of golf with my father (which gained me admission to the after-game chatter at the nineteenth hole), and I could beat nearly anyone at poker. But it was dancing with one of the boys that wrenched me out of my childhood world and into young adulthood.

I was never a good dancer but the repetitive moves of square dancing — the swinging, twirling, tapping and clapping — were something I loved. I was definitely attracted to boys, preferring their company as they did so many more interesting things than we girls did. With boys we sat around and smoked cigarettes while we cooked sausages and potatoes over a fire out in the old gold diggings, we raced bikes down steep sheep tracks at dangerous speeds, dug caves, went fishing in the dams and built huts out of rubbish.

I left school after sitting School Certificate at the age of sixteen and by February 1963 I was employed as second cook at the Ranfurly Hospital.

Everything changed for me in July of that year, a week after my seventeenth birthday.

It was the middle of a Central Otago winter, with snow covering the surrounding mountains and farmland, ponds and dams frozen over, and ice skating and curling in full swing. The Hawkdun and Mt Ida ranges, the Lammermoors and Kakanuis, like tussock-covered sentinels, surrounded the Maniototo Plain. We grew up loving the mountains, the wide-open spaces with soaring hawks, and especially the freedom to roam around the old gold diggings. We would bike for miles from one wee township to another without fear, as we all knew one another.

Up until this time I had had a few boyfriends but no one serious. There was little opportunity to 'go out' with a boyfriend anyway. You could go and watch each other play sports on Saturday if your game times didn't clash and if you were playing in the same town. You could go to the movies together in Ranfurly, and you could go to the monthly dances.

At the movies we would hold hands and snuggle under a boy's arm. That arm would frequently sneak across your shoulder and make a hopeful move down towards your breast. I was short and had a small build with a flat chest; my 'trainer bra' did nothing to enhance my bust. Small breasts were an advantage when playing hockey or tennis, but an embarrassment when it came to boyfriends. We would kiss in the dark with mouths closed, fumbling in our awkward inexperience. A hand placed just above my knee was breathtakingly exciting but also filled me with apprehension.

I vividly remember the first time I was introduced to a 'dry run'. It was after a hockey game, behind the dressing sheds. I had played well and felt good; my boyfriend was all smiles and commented on my good passes from the wing to the centre. We were standing with our backs to the wooden shed, out of sight of everyone, when he leaned towards me and started to rub his body against mine. I could feel his erection, and his breathing was rapid, and then as quickly as it had started, it was all over. I wondered out loud, 'What was that?' He looked embarrassed and muttered 'Sorry' as he turned and walked away. Our relationship came to an abrupt end.

My two friends Lyn and Sue worked at the hospital, and the three of us went to the dances together each month, travelling in Sue's boyfriend's big six-seater car. One night in July, wrapped up in tartan rugs, wearing woollen gloves and with scarves pulled up over our heads, we headed off.

The dance had already started when we pulled up beside other vehicles, including small buses, all lined up in tidy rows outside the hall. Boys stood at one end of the cosy hall, many clutching glasses of warm beer and smoking. The girls sat around the hall on hard seats, chatting, laughing and waiting to be asked for a dance.

By nine o'clock the dance was in full swing, the four-piece band hammering out 'Limbo Rock', 'It's Now or Never', 'Big Girls Don't Cry' and, of course, the Scottish songs 'The White Heather Club' and 'A Scottish Soldier'.

Incredibly, one of the local heartthrobs had asked me to dance with him. He was two years older than me: tall, with sandy-coloured hair and a cute half-smile, plus he was a great dancer. He spun me around, threw me out to the length of his arm and then pulled me back towards him in a very possessive manner, all the time moving his feet in perfect time to the music. I was enthralled: it was exhilarating and exciting as I responded to the music, his closeness saturating me.

When the music stopped, he held my hand tightly. 'Let's go outside, Ruth.'

With no hesitation I let him lead me through the crowd, out into the cold air. I couldn't understand why he had picked me out of all the girls who obviously wanted to dance with him and be seen with him. I felt incredibly special.

'We all came to the dance in the bus; it's over here. Let's go inside out of the cold,' he suggested.

The small bus was parked in the second row of vehicles. There was no lighting outside the hall apart from the weak yellow light cast by the solitary lightbulb above the door. As we climbed the few steps into the bus, a voice called out from the back, 'What have we got here, Warren?' I suddenly felt scared. I tried to let go of Warren's hand but he gripped mine even harder. 'Nothing to worry about,' he told me. 'Just a couple of my mates. Come on, let's sit here.'

I was sitting with my back to the window. Warren was

beside me, and Stewart and Simon, two boys I also knew, were sitting behind us. I instinctively knew I was being set up for something so I tried to stand up, but two hands behind me pushed me back down.

'I would like to get off the bus, please,' I said.

'Please! Well, we would like you to stay, *please*,' replied Stewart, laughing.

I looked straight at Warren and slowly stood up. 'Let me pass.'

Simon, who was sitting behind me, suddenly stood up, leaned forward and put his arm around my neck. Warren then grabbed my arm and pulled me out of the seat and towards the back of the bus. Simon then moved in behind me. He still had one arm around my neck but now his other arm was tight around my waist. I kicked backwards, felt contact with a leg, and heard a yell and a curse in response. I kicked again and at the same time tried to pull away from Warren. I remember being pushed and pulled onto the long seat at the back of the bus, forced down by the weight of Warren.

I must have been screaming because Stewart told me to shut up as he pushed a handkerchief into my mouth. My shoes were thrown off as I continued to struggle and kick. I don't remember what was being said as my mind was in chaos; there was so much happening at once.

I felt as though I was fighting for my life but only had my brain to save me, as my arms, head and legs were being held down. My mind ran through the only possibilities I had. If I struggled they might hurt me more. If I didn't struggle they might think I had given in and therefore agreed to have sex. If I went limp they may think I had fainted and let me go. Maybe I could pretend to have a seizure . . . I wished I had my period, as that might have put them off.

Warren tore off my underwear and was on top of me, looking straight at me, his face so close to mine I could smell beer on his breath. I stared straight back at him. I wanted him to always remember what he had done and that I, the girl underneath him, had witnessed every minute of it. As much as I wanted to shut my eyes to black out what I knew was coming next, I forced myself not to. My mind was shouting 'SEE ME! SEE ME! SEE ME!'

I remember the pain. My mouth was full and dry from the handkerchief; I felt I might choke. Simon was kneeling on my arms, which were pulled up over my head. One of my legs was being held, the other pushed up against the back of the seat. I went limp.

Fog. Grey fog. Black fog. Red fog.

My eyes were open but I couldn't focus. Just faces glaring at me, contorted with emotions I couldn't work out. Lust, hatred, control, or even loss of control?

I remember my tears, so many that the whole side of my face was wet. I felt as though I was being ripped apart. Someone was repeating 'GO, man, GO!' Warren collapsed and lifted himself off me, as a strong repulsive smell settled around me. I was wet between the legs. I had lost all sense of time.

The three of them stood up, ignoring me. Simon pulled the handkerchief out of my mouth and then I was alone. I heard the bus door open and close, followed by a hollow silence.

———

THE REST OF that night and the next day are like a jigsaw puzzle dropped and broken on the floor. I have never put all the pieces back together. Yes, I did go back into the hall, but for how long? What did I do? Were the three boys there? I don't remember. What did I tell my friends?

My next clear thought is of cleaning myself in the bathroom at the Nurses' Home, putting on a sanitary belt and towel as I was still bleeding, washing out my underwear and throwing my stockings in the rubbish bin.

The next day was a Sunday so I had the day off work. What I did that morning, the morning after, I can't recall. How did I even get home that night? Maybe I rang Mum, maybe I hitched — I don't know. But I do remember that Mum instinctively knew something was wrong, as she put me straight to bed fully clothed. She rang the matron at the hospital and said I was sick and wouldn't be in for a few days.

Did she guess what had happened before I told her? A decade later I would finally ask her that question, when I was nursing her as she died of cancer.

'I'm your mother; I knew something had happened,' she said. 'But I wasn't prepared for what you told me.' Mum was only about 37 when I was raped, a young mother of two teenage girls with no family support, except Dad, as all of our relations still lived in Christchurch.

My next recollection is of Mum waking me and telling me she had run me a bath. I went into the bathroom and sank into the warm water. It was then that I noticed the bruises on my shoulders, arms and legs.

'I'll come and wash your hair if you want,' called Mum.

'No, I can do it,' I responded quickly, but she came in anyway. Without saying a word she started to wash me, ever so gently.

It was so quiet, just the sound of the water. I started to cry; Mum held me and then she was crying with me. I was sobbing, choking, my whole body shaking.

My mother was small, with red hair and a beautiful smile. She was nicknamed Fred, short for Freda. She was a brilliant mother.

'We're going to have to talk about this, Ruthie.'

I nodded. She rubbed me dry, helped me dress and then combed my hair. 'It is going to be all right. It will be okay. Let's just get today over.'

Mum told me, all those years later, that she wanted

time to prepare Dad. She was worried he would 'line the bastards up and shoot them'.

On the Monday, Mum took me to see Dr McQueen in Ranfurly. After the examination he spoke to my mother alone as I sat with his nurse in reception. I was sure we would be going to the police station next, but we didn't.

Dad hardly spoke to me in the aftermath of the rape. He was quiet and downcast. One memory I have of Dad is that every morning we could hear him whistling and singing as he worked in the butcher shop adjoining our home. After the rape he stopped whistling and singing. The house was quiet.

I went back to work. By now I was first cook, cooking for the staff and patients of the whole hospital.

A week or so later, Mum told me that Dad had been to see Warren's father and everything had been 'dealt with'. The police would not be involved. I have never known what exactly happened or what was discussed, but the awful outcome was that Warren's father gave Dad £50, which was passed on to me. The crisp banknote didn't solve anything; it only raised raw, hurtful questions. Was that the going price for the rape, or my silence? I was incredibly angry. It was a rage that I would carry inside of me for years.

After missing two periods, I knew I was pregnant. When Mum and I told my father he left the house, walked down to the Ancient Briton Hotel and got drunk. Abortion was never discussed. I was to continue working until

December. It was heavy, hard work, with long hours and huge responsibility for a pregnant seventeen-year-old.

No one outside the family was told I was pregnant. It was common, back then, for pregnant girls to be sent away to another part of the country to have their babies, and to come back afterwards as though nothing had happened. Adoption of the babies was accepted as the obvious and easiest solution. Babies were taken from the mothers as soon as they were born, the reasoning being that if the mother never saw her child she would recover mentally more quickly.

I was to go up to Wellington in January, as I could no longer hide my expanding tummy. I travelled by train to Lyttelton and then by the interisland ferry across Cook Strait to the capital, where I lived with my Aunty Joyce and Uncle Bill.

The red £50 note was handed over to them. I still think of that note as blood money.

My son was born on 10 April 1964. I was never allowed to see him.

Four years later, on 10 April 1968, the Lyttelton–Wellington ferry *Wahine* ran aground in Wellington Harbour. As people witnessed the horrendous maritime disaster resulting in the deaths of 52 people, all I could think was that it was my son's fourth birthday.

CHAPTER 6

OFF TO
THE NAVY

I returned home to Naseby as though nothing had happened. It was the start of my life of lies. This happened to so many young girls in the 1960s and 70s, as having a baby out of wedlock was simply unacceptable. We all learnt to live with it. What do you say when you are asked questions you cannot answer truthfully? 'Where have you been? Have you been working in Wellington? You must have had a great time — why come back to Naseby?' I didn't even know whether my cousins or aunties had been told that I had been away to have a baby; that part of my life seemed to have been totally erased. I didn't even know if my sister knew.

Before all this happened, I had been accepted into the navy. Obviously it had to be delayed, but then I was informed that I could join in August 1964 as a sick berth attendant, signing up initially for three years. Everything was very strained at home — conversation no longer flowed easily and I knew Mum was carrying most of the load. I had to get away. Joining the navy was the obvious answer.

'She'll be all right once she gets up there,' I heard Dad say to Mum.

The idea of being a Wren (member of the Women's Royal Naval Service) interested me, but more than that, getting away up to a new life in Auckland was the final step towards total denial of what had happened to me. I travelled by train from Ranfurly to Dunedin, then another train from Dunedin to Picton. I crossed Cook Strait on the ferry, then travelled by overnight train from Wellington to Auckland, a fourteen-hour journey.

My life was now full of structure. You had to be in uniform, on time; to pay attention, stand to attention, salute and say 'Yes, ma'am' and 'No, sir'. Because many of the regulations didn't make sense to me, I questioned everything in the beginning, quickly discovering that challenging the system got you punished. Extra duties and cancellation of leave became common punishments during my very short naval career. My navy history sheet states: 'Having trouble settling down. Capable but not committed . . . Takes time for Senior personnel to gain her confidence.'

After initial training we were moved to Elizabeth House on King Edward Parade, Devonport. Originally built as the Ventnor Hotel, it offered the Wrens top accommodation overlooking the sparkling Auckland Harbour. It had a massive kitchen and dining room, big bathrooms and a beautiful staircase. The bedrooms, called cabins, had to be kept spotlessly clean: 'No books to be left on the bedside table, Wren!' was a command I was given more than once.

I learnt to drive with money that Gran had given me when I turned eighteen, the driving instructor picking me up at the gates of HMNZS *Philomel*. I don't know how she managed it but Gran had banked one shilling a month for both Jill and me from the time we were born until we left school. Jill bought Gran an electric toaster with her money and I paid for my driving lessons. Dad then bought me a Ford Prefect, which he shipped up to Auckland — I was one of the few Wrens who owned a car and I felt very proud.

Gran died while I was in the navy. I was excused from hospital duty for the day but was denied compassionate leave, so I could not attend the funeral in Christchurch. That was the first time I asked myself what I was doing in the navy. I started to think about dating for the first time since the rape, but as a precaution I first signed up for a self-defence course being held in Devonport. The instructor asked me, 'What exactly brings you here?'

'I want to stop being scared.'

'What are you scared of?'

'Men. Being raped.'

'Have you been raped?'

I looked him straight in the eye and replied, 'Yes.'

It was never mentioned again. I think some of the other women on the course must have given similar answers, as our instructor was clearly committed to helping us. From the first night we were comprehensively drilled in basic survival and self-defence skills.

'You are *never* to feel afraid again as you now have the ability to defend yourselves,' he stated firmly. He taught us how to fall with the punches, using the attacker's own strength to get them off balance. 'Don't run at the start, because you'll be caught. Get yourself into a position where you can ball him — and then run.'

He showed us what he meant, and it made complete sense. A few quick lessons on how to position ourselves and maintain balance, and then the ace card — 'Grab the balls, half twist and pull!' he yelled. 'Repeat after me! Grab the balls, half twist and pull!' We practised pulling on a sock he held on his thigh, which had two balls in it — somewhat bigger than normal testicles but we soon got the idea. We all started laughing while doing the 'ball' move. Slowly, we regained our confidence.

At the end of the course I was no longer scared. Boyfriends could now be back on the agenda, as I had the ace card.

———

NURSING AT THE naval hospital was something I really enjoyed. We attended lectures each morning during the first year, studying from the 508-page *Handbook of the Royal Navy Sick Berth Staff*, published in London in 1959. This covered many of the -ologies and diseases, impending death, surgery, dental surgery, psychiatry, pharmacology and toxicology. We carried out practical ward work in the women's ward, the men's ward, a surgical ward, an operating theatre and a tiny isolation ward. Our training covered everything a sick berth attendant (SBA) might need to know if sent to sea. So, why, after three years, did we come out with *no* qualifications? Why could we not link in to the main Auckland hospital and study towards becoming registered nurses? Why did we never actually go to sea like the men did? From 1986 women finally were allowed to serve at sea, initially on non-combatant ships and subsequently on all types of ships.

I had been recommended to sit for Leading Wren but I wasn't interested. Matron Brown took me off ward duties and placed me in theatre; she believed I had the ability to be a good operating theatre nurse and hoped I would get stuck in and settle down. I really tried to be good, but as my grandmother had said many years before, I just couldn't.

After two and a half years of the restrictions and limitations of military life, one morning I just packed up my Ford Prefect and headed south. I was going home. The navy police rang Dad and told him I was AWOL, and if I turned up in Naseby he was to contact them immediately. Not one to be intimidated, Dad replied, 'If she gets home, she can stay home. She obviously doesn't want to be in the navy if she has left!'

Luck was with me for my drive down the North Island but they caught up with me at the ferry terminal. Two navy police, dressed in full naval uniform, arrested me. It was quite a scene. Then the three of us piled into my tiny car and I was ordered to drive us all back to Devonport!

On our arrival my car was locked in the commander's garage and I was placed under open arrest. This meant I was not sent to prison but I had a military policeman stationed outside my cabin door at night, who also accompanied me to work at the hospital every day. I had to report to the officer on duty at 2359 every night in full blues. I received double duties and no pay for a time, and leave was cancelled for six months. I was the first Wren and possibly the only female to go AWOL. I had told my defending officer I never intended to complete my three years and therefore was not AWOL, but this turned out to be exactly the wrong thing to say. I was quickly informed that I could be charged with desertion, which was much worse.

As I walked around base I was openly called a 'skate', which basically meant someone who was not only a slippery fish but who also avoided hard work. I knew I was neither.

After a short time, I was permitted to make a request to the commodore for discharge. Accompanied by my defending officer, Petty Officer Collins, I was marched into a room to stand on a mat in front of the commodore, who stood behind a small desk. I saluted, stated my name, rank and number, then my request. As I was under punishment, my request for discharge had a slim chance of being granted.

And indeed it was not. I don't remember how many times I fronted the commodore but finally he relented and I was discharged. He told me how disappointed he was with me and how I had let the navy down, especially the Wrens. I would never make anything of myself, he said. His criticism bounced right off — he didn't know me!

It was November 1966 and my naval career was over, the highlight being the day I spent on the American submarine *Archerfish*, becoming an honorary submariner because we had submerged in the Hauraki Gulf.

The day after I left, a navy friend gave me a two-year-old German shepherd named Rewa. He thought I needed not only company for the long trip back home, but also some protection. I loaded up the back of my wee Ford Prefect, Rewa sitting alert and excited on the front seat, and I drove out of Auckland. We were away, heading south — as south as you could get in fact — off to Stewart Island, where Mum and Dad were now running the Oban Hotel.

TALES FROM
THE BOOKSHOPS:
GREEN BOOKS ONLY

———

MY FIRST BOOKSHOP in Manapōuri, 45 South and Below, was very well known in the area. The walls were home to a growing number of books displayed on an array of bookshelves, some professionally made, and others nailed together by Lance.

A middle-aged lady came into the shop one day and without any greeting she started to collect together books with green spines. Her pile grew as she stripped my shelves. I thought it was a little strange, and surely not coincidence.

'This is an interesting collection of books,' I said eventually. 'Are you aware that some of them are rare . . . and quite . . . expensive?'

'Oh, I'm not worried about the cost,' she replied. 'Only the colour. I have a new home and want to colour-coordinate the library.' She smiled when she said this.

I had never heard of a colour-coordinated library. I stood looking at her in total disbelief. After about 20 seconds of stunned silence I managed to blurt out, 'Well, my books have to be read! I will not sell any of my books just to be put in a fake library and forgotten. You can't buy any of these books!'

'I'm willing to pay for them!' she replied, taken aback.

'Well, I'm not going to sell them,' I said sharply, and started to put the books back on the shelves.

She gathered up her things and stormed out of the shop.

A colour-coordinated library?! Not with my books!

CHAPTER 7

STEWART ISLAND AND MEETING LANCE

Dad had seen an advertisement in the paper for a manager to run the Oban Hotel on Stewart Island and successfully applied for the position. Mum and Dad were off on another adventure — managing a near-bankrupt hotel after the previous manager had just walked out one day and left the island.

They crossed Foveaux Strait by ferry from Bluff, with Beswick the cat and Floyd the bird. The first thing Dad did was sack everyone on the spot. I can just hear him saying, 'Okay, you buggers, pack your bags. Holiday time is over!'

The hotel was spring-cleaned, new staff were employed, a small garden was planted out the front and they reopened.

Mum took over the accommodation and restaurant side of the business and Dad ran the bar. He was in his element, serving beer, playing cards; sometimes he played two or three games of euchre at a time, all lined up along the bar. After a year of silence, he was singing and whistling again.

I arrived on the island with my newly adopted dog Rewa, and was immediately employed as cook. There was no electricity on the island back then — everyone had generators that were switched off at night, and we nearly all cooked on coal ranges as gas was very expensive. Everything was brought across to the island by ferry, or occasionally by float-plane from Invercargill.

The massive coal range in the hotel's kitchen was wonderful to cook on, but it meant starting early in the morning to get the heat up in time for breakfast. Tradesmen — from what we called 'the mainland' — stayed at the hotel during the week and went home on weekends, so we catered for them as well as the tourists who came across on day trips. If the weather was bad we would only prepare for a small number of visitors, as many of them arrived seasick and spent their four-hour stay on the island sitting in the lounge, mentally preparing themselves for the trip back.

When we were busy, Mum would help Rita, our waitress, in the dining room. On one rather busy day Mum came running into the kitchen holding her top dentures — they were in two pieces, split perfectly in half. We quickly glued them back together and put them in the oven to dry. Dad came storming into the kitchen, frowning . . . not a good sign. 'People are waiting for their meals. Come on, hurry up!' Then he noticed Mum had no top teeth. 'Don't worry,' he said. 'Just don't talk or smile. We're here to feed them, not entertain them!' We took the teeth out of the oven, ran cold water over them and Mum was up and running as though nothing had happened.

Each evening I would peel the potatoes for the next day, filling a huge pot and placing a lump of coal in the soaking water, which kept the potatoes white. I could make scones, apple sponge, pikelets, madeira and chocolate cake without having to measure the ingredients; carve meat, batter fish, and throw together a quick meal for any of the workers who came in late.

I turned 21 on Stewart Island. Mum sent out very formal-looking invitations:

> Requesting the pleasure of the
> company of . . . on the occasion
> of the 21st birthday of Ruth at the
> Oban Hotel . . .

Mum and Dad gave me a transistor radio, there were telegrams from absent friends, and a few of the invited locals joined us for dinner after the party. Mum had written up a special menu on the Oban Hotel's letterhead paper, and Dad generously opened two bottles of sparkling Corbans Premiere Cuvée.

By this time Dad had the bar humming; the hotel was now the hub of the small fishing community.

Three major events happened in 1967. First, there was New Zealand's introduction of decimal currency in July. In October, 50 years of the 'six o'clock swill' ended, with 67 per cent of voters supporting ten o'clock closing of pubs. Also that month, on Black Friday, the following short note appeared in the local news-sheet:

> *Late News: Mr L Shaw and*
> *Miss R Hobday are engaged.*

I had met the love of my life.

———

LANCE SHAW WAS a fisherman, working for Micky Squires on the *Rosalind*, crayfishing and trawling east of Lords River. He wore thigh gumboots and jeans, and had a beard and dark hair. Occasionally he would come into the hotel for a drink. Rita and I would watch him walking down to the wharf or to the only shop on the island, across the road from the hotel. He was the best-looking guy on the island.

Every once in a while there would be a dance at the

small community hall, attended mainly by fishermen and their wives, the single fishermen and the very few single girls. One such night I saw Lance sitting on the floor, back against the wall, playing a red guitar while a woman with big breasts lounged beside him. I don't think he even noticed me that first night; I had no such breasts to catch his attention!

Neither of us can remember our first date but we soon started to see each other regularly. At last I felt that something was very real in my life — I was in love. Lance faced the wrath of Dad on many occasions over the next year, always responding with his trademark polite and gentle manner. Mum loved Lance, but Dad went into King Peacock mode when it came to his daughters.

———

AN AIR SERVICE to Stewart Island had begun in March 1951, and by October that year two aircraft were running from Invercargill, also servicing Lake Wakatipu and Lake Te Anau and giving access to many remote, unknown parts of Fiordland. Five new lakes were discovered and over 120 landing locations were selected in 52 approved waterways.

It was a very big occasion when quizmaster Selwyn Toogood visited Stewart Island in October 1968. He was known throughout New Zealand for his television show, *It's In The Bag*. A large crowd gathered on the beach as the float-plane came flying in, bringing the famously big man with the big personality. As the plane approached, we noticed that the wheels were down; then we watched in horror as it nose-dived when it hit the water.

The force of water smashed the windscreen, and white spray quickly covered the plane and surged into the cabin. Then it disappeared from sight . . . We were all aghast, then relieved when the plane resurfaced — upside down. Some fishermen raced to their dinghies and started to row out to the plane while the passengers hung suspended by their safety belts, heads only a few inches above the water.

The pilot was quick to extricate himself and helped the passengers clamber out and into the dinghies — except for Selwyn Toogood. The poor man was too large to haul himself up out of the hatchway. We watched anxiously from the beach as the plane slowly started to sink, while two men leapt up beside the hatch and, with great effort, pulled him out. Our famous visitor had arrived in a very unceremonious fashion!

He needed dry clothing but Mum couldn't find anything on the island big enough to fit him. The community hall was packed to watch the show that night, with everyone talking about the float-plane incident. Selwyn strode onto the stage with a huge smile and we all cheered and clapped. He was wrapped in a blanket that Mum had pinned together with safety pins, and, without the benefit of his glasses, he cheerily welcomed everyone and entertained us as though nothing had happened.

———

I WAS STILL a Catholic and wanted to marry in a Catholic church, so once a fortnight Lance met with the visiting priest who came over from Invercargill. In its 'Instruction on Mixed Marriage', the Code of Canon Law stated:

> *The non-Catholic party, with appropriate delicacy but also in clear terms, should be informed about the Catholic doctrine regarding the dignity of marriage, and especially about its principal properties, name[ly] unity and indissolubility. The non-Catholic party should also be informed about the grave obligation for the Catholic spouse to protect, preserve, and practise his or her own faith and to baptise and educate any offspring to be born in the same faith.*

It was this final sentence that tipped everything over the edge. All Lance wanted to do was marry me. He reluctantly agreed to become a Catholic, but it wasn't until the very last day of instruction that the priest told him his children would also have to be raised in the Catholic faith. Lance has always been extremely honest and he just couldn't agree to this. His children would have the freedom to choose their own paths, not have it preordained by a religion he didn't even believe in himself.

My mother had become a Catholic to marry Dad, so Jill and I were brought up as Catholics. I felt that if I left the faith I would be letting her down — I was still blindly immersed in Catholic ways. There was no way for us to compromise on this matter and so we reached an impasse. Our engagement was over.

By now my wedding dress was made, the invitations had been printed (but not sent out), our wedding rings had been made out of gold from Dad's mine, and the church was booked. When everything fell apart so fast we were both stunned. I was torn apart and Lance immediately left the island, shattered.

Not long after, I repacked my car and headed north to Wellington. The act of packing my bags and moving on after a calamity was already becoming a theme of my young life.

It would be twenty years before I saw Lance again.

TALES FROM THE BOOKSHOPS: HOW NOT TO READ A BOOK

——

AN ELDERLY COUPLE came into my bookshop, and after a brief hello they settled into what appeared to be a practised routine to hunt out the book they wanted. The gentleman stayed outside and methodically went through the books on the tables and bookstands, while his wife perused all the books on the shelves inside, guided with a pointed finger. They were quiet and very focused. After some time they came together by the counter, each clasping a book to their chest, with matching looks of delight in their eyes.

'What do you think of this, Arthur? It is a bit of a love story but it's a gutsy book — *Eleven Minutes* by Paulo Coelho.'

Arthur looked at the book, flicked through it, read the blurb on the cover and handed it back. 'Not our usual type of read. Are you happy with it?'

'He's a bestselling author, so yes, I'm interested.'

I wondered if she realised that the premise of the love story was, in fact, hiding the extremely emotional story of a young prostitute.

'Good, so that's one. Now, look what I've found, Joyce,' said Arthur, handing his wife the book he held.

'Another war story,' Joyce observed, with barely concealed disappointment.

'It'll be an easy read. What do you think?'

'Yes, let's go with these two.' Decision made.

By now a few questions were bobbing about in my mind. 'So you both read all the books you buy together?'

'Oh yes, that's what makes it so interesting — we discuss every book,' Joyce answered.

'Do you ever stop reading a book once you've started it?'

Arthur looked at me with astonishment. 'No. No, that's never happened. We read every book.'

'What about books you don't really enjoy?' I asked. 'Now that I'm over 70, if a book doesn't capture me within a few chapters I put it aside. I don't have time to read all the books I want to; I can't waste time reading something I don't enjoy.'

'It's not a problem for us — we have a system,' Arthur said. 'Joyce reads the first hundred pages of the book and I read the last hundred pages. We then discuss the book and fill in the middle.'

It took me a while to wrap my head around what he was saying. Joyce stood beside him, nodding in agreement. 'It works well,' she said. 'And it means we have time to read more books.' They estimated they got through five books a week.

'But what about the storyline?' I asked. 'New characters might be introduced, or there may be an incredible plot twist in the middle, or someone at the beginning of the book could be killed off halfway through and not even mentioned at the end of the book . . .'

Joyce interrupted me. 'It doesn't matter, really. We fill in the story.'

I took their $8, and as I placed it in the Blind Foundation's collection box, I said, 'I really will have to think about your book-reading technique. I'm glad it works for you. Would you like me to tell you a little about the middle of *Eleven Minutes*?'

'Oh *no*!' they both exclaimed immediately. 'You'll spoil the whole story!'

CHAPTER
8

WORKING FOR THE ARCHBISHOP

I stopped driving when I reached Wellington and stayed with my aunty and uncle for a few days while I looked for work. It was 1968. I had lived with them while I was pregnant so they were used to caring for me as I patched my life back together. My wonderful Aunty Joyce was, as usual, full of sympathy. 'Oh, Ruthie, I was so sure you had settled down. Lance sounded so wonderful.' Uncle offered his own version of support: 'Up with the anchor again then, love?'

I applied for the position of cook for the priests at the Sacred Heart Presbytery in Guildford Terrace, Thorndon. Father Bernard 'Totty' Tottman interviewed me and said I was certainly qualified for the job, but he was concerned about my age, as I was only 22. The women who worked in presbyteries were usually a lot older than me, and as there were four young priests in residence he said he would have to discuss it with Archbishop McKeefry.

The next day Totty confirmed I had the position. I moved into my self-contained flat at the back of the presbytery and started cooking for six hungry men. Kath was the housekeeper, an elderly woman who came in very early every morning so she could go to Mass before work. She lived for her work and was extremely protective of the priests. Initially she found it difficult having a young woman working in the kitchen, but eventually we became good friends (even though I didn't go to Mass every day!).

Totty was a delight. He ran the presbytery in a calm, fatherly way, full of encouragement for everyone. I spring-cleaned the kitchen and dining room, rearranged the pantry, and introduced everyone to my experimental cooking, which they loved.

Archbishop McKeefry would breakfast by himself as he preferred to eat later than the others. I would serve him, and often sit at the other end of the big table and chat to him. He said I had brought sunshine to the house, and he enjoyed the way I sang while I was working. I never told him about Lance; it still hurt too much to talk about him. The Archbishop asked me why I didn't have a boyfriend. 'Why come and cook for us, Ruth? Perhaps you are going to be a nun. Have you ever thought about that?' I admit I had considered it, albeit briefly!

On Kath's days off I made the Archbishop's bed and tidied his office. In his wardrobe hung a few beautifully embroidered vestments and a mitre (bishop's hat), folded flat on top of an internal set of drawers. I just couldn't stop myself — I placed the mitre on my head and stood looking at myself in the long mirror.

'Doesn't really suit you, Ruth — looks too big.' There was the Archbishop, standing at the door with a big grin. 'Maybe you are too short to wear a hat like that?'

——

IN EARLY DECEMBER I made the Christmas pudding, storing it in the pantry and feeding it every few days with brandy. It smelt wonderful. Christmas was a remarkably busy time for the priests: people dropping in with presents, visiting priests and nuns, additional masses, rosary, extra choir practices, home visits, and more parishioners than usual coming to confession.

Christmas dinner was at 12.30: a four-course meal at a beautifully decorated table with a present for each priest. I was at a loss as to what to buy for the Archbishop; I ended up getting him two goldfish in a big bowl full of water, weed and rocks. Aunty Joyce was appalled. 'Ruth, you can't give an Archbishop goldfish for Christmas!'

'Aunty,' I replied, 'have you ever tried to buy an archbishop a Christmas present?'

Over Christmas dinner there was lots of laughter, drinking of wine and opening of presents. The Archbishop was delighted with the goldfish, much to the surprise of everyone except me. Finally it was time for the Christmas pudding, to be served with brandy sauce and cream. I heated brandy in a deep soup ladle over the gas, carried it into the dining room and poured it over the pudding. The Archbishop was waiting with a match to light it. As the flame hit the pudding it went off like a small bomb, blue flames leaping around the entire pudding and down onto the plate. Totty panicked and threw his linen napkin over the flames. The napkin turned black but it did put the fire out. Once the shock was over, we all burst out laughing. I was just relieved the Archbishop hadn't burnt his holy hand. I was invited to sit and join them to eat the sensational pudding.

On 30 December I received a letter from the Archbishop:

> At this time of the year it is usual for me to announce to the priests the various transfers and appointments for the coming year. It is not usual to transfer housekeepers . . . Accordingly I have decided not to transfer you but to ask you to be so kind as to stay at Sacred Heart for another year.

I have always believed that the priests, especially the young ones, should be provided with the best of food, and plenty of it. I want you to take special notice of this point in the coming year, and to see that the members of the household and all those who visit us from time to time are treated with the best the house has to offer.

I know that this has been your policy since you came here and ask you to maintain, and if possible to surpass it in the year ahead. I am very conscious of the high quality of the priests associated with me in the house, so I rely on you to give them the greatly honoured treatment such wonderful fellows deserve.

Yours sincerely in Christ

The Archbishop

I stayed until April the following year. By this time the Archbishop had become New Zealand's first cardinal, and I could feel the ever-growing need to keep moving. Totty wrote a glowing reference, the young priests hugged me goodbye, and I set off on my next adventure: sailing around the Pacific.

TALES FROM THE BOOKSHOPS: TRACTOR LIFE

———

GEORGE IS OUR local chemist. His pharmacy, which he runs with his wife Michelle, is in Te Anau, a twenty-minute drive from Manapōuri. He used to fly aeroplanes as a hobby, but after a rather spectacular crash, which he says made him 'sore!', he took up yachting, crewing for Lance on his Noelex 22.

George and Michelle built a house on a one-and-a-half-hectare property just out of Te Anau, and this presented an opportunity for George to buy a Ferguson TEA tractor, similar to the one Sir Edmund Hillary took to Antarctica. He bought it from a charlatan in Queenstown who, apparently, had dragged it out of a hedge and painted it red, rather than the recognisable grey.

George mostly uses his tractor to shuttle stuff around, enjoying the engine noise while he bounces along, dreaming of being retired in fourteen years' time. He has bought a grubber and is now looking for a set of mounted discs so he can establish a vegetable garden, his dream being to start growing massive quantities of vegetables. He aims to become 'the broccoli — or potato — man for Te Anau'.

He has read his favourite book, *The Garden in the Clouds: Confessions of a hopeless romantic*, winner of the National Trust Outdoor Book of the Year in 2011, at least four times. The author, Antony Woodward, purchased Tair-Ffynnon, a derelict smallholding 400 metres up in the Black Mountains of Wales. He tells the story of his incredibly ambitious dream to create, *in one year*, in the mountainous Welsh landscape, a garden fit for inclusion in the prestigious 'yellow book' — the *Gardens of England and Wales Open for Charity* guide.

George loved Woodward's book because the author not only had a tractor but did so many things that were bonkers, maybe a little like George himself. I also loved this book, as it is written with humour and is full of very interesting facts and stories.

George was looking for another book to read and the obvious choice for him was the award-winning *A Short History of Tractors in Ukrainian* by Marina Lewycka. It is about Nikolai, an 84-year-old Ukrainian man who falls in love with young Valentina, also Ukrainian. A marriage takes place, stimulating some sexual fantasies that are quite beyond Nikolai's physical capabilities. Throughout the book there are short chapters on the history of the tractor, a book Nikolai is writing. I knew George would love this book.

I am convinced there is a book for everyone, and it amazes me how often that perfect book is on a shelf in my Wee Bookshop with fewer than 1000 titles.

ALL
ABOARD

As happy as I had been working at the presbytery, I was still trying to outrun my growing despair over the difficult past few years of my life. All I could do was keep moving and keep ahead of the panicked swirl of thoughts in my head that threatened to overwhelm me if I stayed put for too long.

What had happened to Lance? And what had happened to my son? The 1955 Adoption Act meant I could not lawfully try to find my son until he was 21 — a lifetime away. A growing hunger was gnawing at me. I would see the face of an unknown child in a crowd and wonder if *that* young boy was mine. Much later, I would find out that all the time I was in Wellington, my son, who had been adopted by a Catholic family, was living only ten minutes away. But at this stage, everything felt claustrophobic. I had to get away, and further than before. The opportunity to leave New Zealand presented the ideal escape from growing despair.

The *Cutty Sark* was a locally famous yacht, named after the nineteenth-century sailing ship and launched in Lyttelton in 1946, the year I was born.

It had been decades in the making. At the age of nineteen, Henry Jones had outlined the project on paper: 60 feet (18 metres) in length, a beam of 12 foot 6 inches (3.8 metres), weighing 48 tons. Eight tons of English oak was ordered from England in 1929, which finally arrived in 1931. It was then toughened by lying for seven years in the sea at Redcliffs, Christchurch. Two Oregon poles were imported from America for the original ketch rig of main mast and mizzen.

The interior included a piano set up beside an open fireplace in the saloon for Henry Jones' wife, and a bath aft off their cabin. All up, it took 23 years to build and cost £30,000.

When I joined as crew in 1969 she was single-masted, Marconi-rigged, with a 44-horse-powered Fordson engine. The sail wardrobe contained eleven sails, including three flax storm sails. The main spinnaker was 2000 square feet (186 square metres) and the reaching spinnaker

1250 square feet (116 square metres). The *Cutty Sark* had been sold to Bill Bradley in 1953. He raced her in the Whangarei-to-Nouméa race and also the Sydney-to-Hobart. In the earliest years of the Sydney–Hobart race all the yachts were built from timber — heavy-displacement cutters, sloops, yawls, schooners and ketches were designed more for cruising than racing, so the *Cutty Sark* fitted in well.

In 1966 Basil Fleming became her owner, and his dream was to sail the Pacific.

We left Wellington on 29 June 1969, the day before my twenty-third birthday. We were between Cape Kidnappers and Napier and I was suffering from a horrid combination of violent seasickness and noisy diarrhoea. I struggled into a safety harness, clipped myself to the aft rail, stripped off my lower clothing and hung my bare bum over the side to be washed by the waves. As I was looking forward, I noticed smoke coming out of the centre hatchway, but I was so sick, the flames could have been scorching my bum and I couldn't have found the energy to shout 'Fire!' I clung to the rail, wide-eyed and naked from the waist down, as two of the guys put the fire out. An oil leak dripping onto a bare wire had caused it. Happy birthday, Ruth!

Our two-day stopover in Napier was a welcome if short-lived relief, as 24 hours after leaving harbour we were hit by a 55-knot southerly gale. This time over half the crew joined me clinging to the rail. But by day three I was over my seasickness, the ocean was calm and the sun was out.

How quickly you can go from wanting to throw yourself overboard to experiencing absolute elation at being alive in the middle of a vast and lazy blue ocean!

I loved deck work, which was exciting, frightening and often dangerous when changing heavy sails. I loved standing watch on a starry night, listening to the ocean and the comforting chatter of the sails and ropes. I felt free for the first time since I was a child.

Over the next four months we sailed with the trade winds to the Cook Islands, through to the Society Islands (including Tahiti, Moorea, Huahine, Raiatea, Tahaa and Bora Bora), over to Palmerston Atoll and then to American Samoa and Western Samoa. The cyclone season in that part of the Pacific runs from November to April so we planned to reach Suva (Fiji) by late October.

It was August when we tied stern to the bank running along the main road of Papeete in Tahiti. I wrote in my diary: 'Received 15 letters. Running out of money, NZ dollar worthless, US dollar 95 francs. Everything is very expensive and hardly anyone speaks English.'

I needed to find a way to earn some money. Crewing was unpaid, and we all had to contribute towards food. My father had told me that solutions to problems were always close by; you only needed to look for opportunities. The market was within walking distance of the boat and I had been there every morning since we arrived to buy fresh fruit, vegetables and fish. The vendors began to recognise me and although we couldn't hold a conversation in English, French or Tahitian I managed to find out the daily cost for a small space on the ground. I had three packs of cards with me; it was time to put them to work.

I set up beside a big Tahitian 'vahine' who was selling shells, carvings and turtle shells. With the help of a young man I wrote my sign in French: 'Jeu de Cartes — Apprenez à jouer au Pontoon!' 'Card game — Learn to play pontoon.' Gambling was illegal so money was not mentioned.

The first morning I taught people how to play pontoon. There was a lot of laughter, which attracted a large crowd. The second morning a group of men were waiting for me to set up the cards. They squatted around me and placed money in front of them, covering it with their loose clothing. There was no discussion — we all knew we were breaking the law. One man smiled at me, his eyes deliberately went from left to right, then he nodded his head. I didn't move, just glanced up slowly and saw that he had placed 'lookouts' around us. He tapped the ground: time to play!

We played for three mornings at the market and then down on the beach late afternoon. By now I had won 5000 francs (US$50) so I bought myself a pair of sandals for 395 francs and a pareo (body wrap) for 250.

Eagerly I arrived at the market on the fourth morning but I knew immediately something was off. My site was empty, no one was waiting to play, and there were no lookouts. I knew I was in trouble. I turned to leave but two gendarmes stopped me, pointing to their vehicle to make it clear that I was under arrest.

As they hadn't *actually* caught me gambling, they arrested me instead for vagrancy. I had only 200 francs on me. My passport had been stamped by immigration on arrival so I was in French Polynesia legally, but I had left it back on the boat. It would have been easy to take me there to get it, but apparently this was not an option. The officer interviewing me spoke English so I asked him if I could ring New Zealand collect, and he could then confirm who I was. He agreed to this. The time difference meant it was about 6 a.m. in New Zealand, but miraculously my father was awake and answered the phone.

'Papeete police here, sir. We have your daughter Ruth in custody. Arrested for vagrancy.'

After a brief discussion the policeman asked my father, 'Do you have the money to pay for her return flight to New Zealand?'

There was a pause, then the officer shook his head, put the phone down and looked across at me in amazement. My father had told him I could look after myself and had hung up! Yes, that was my father. No surprise to me.

'He's right — I can look after myself!' I said sharply. 'Take me back to the boat. You can see my passport and that I have my own money.'

By now the crew had been informed by locals that I

had been arrested and a handful of them turned up at the police station. They testified that I was not a vagrant so I was released, but we were ordered to leave Tahiti. After customs and immigration had cleared us for departure I went to the market to buy food for the 210-kilometre trip to Huahine. I found my gambling friends, slipped one of them a pack of cards and quickly said my goodbyes.

It was a long haul of six days at sea from Bora Bora back to Aitutaki, with light winds and very hot days. My diary reads:

> When we came ashore, we were told a little boy aged nine had just been dragged out of the water. I rushed over, couldn't feel a pulse, cleared his throat and started mouth to mouth. I continued until a doctor arrived who pronounced him dead. Extremely upset.

The following entry:

> I had to write a statement at 0830 and then attend the inquest at 1300 followed by the funeral at 1430. He was buried in a small grave in their front garden. The family were very kind to me, wanting to give me gifts. I can't stop crying.

IT WAS WHEN we were in American Samoa that we first met up with the large wooden Swedish vessel *Svanen* (meaning 'swan') and her nine crew. Like us, they were on route to Suva for the cyclone season, via the Samoan islands and Niuafo'ou, the northernmost Tongan island.

Peter, a journalist from Australia, was one of the crew on the *Svanen*. Over the next month he and I became very close, exploring the islands together, and staying ashore together whenever possible. When we arrived in Suva he moved onto the *Cutty Sark*, when the entire crew of the *Svanen* walked off the boat.

We sailed the *Cutty Sark* onto the government slip in Suva, as she was in need of repairs — 'slipping' is a process whereby the boat is pulled out of the water for repairs and/ or maintenance. Peter and I had decided to fly to Brisbane together after the *Cutty Sark* was back in the water, as we both needed paid work. To my surprise, he asked me to marry him. 'Why wait?' he said. 'Let's get married straight away!'

The next afternoon we headed out to sea, together with five crew and Bazil, the skipper from the *Cutty Sark*. It was a short ceremony: I wore a casual white dress and a huge smile as we exchanged vows. It wasn't legally binding, but we planned on having a formal wedding when we were settled in Australia.

I rang home and told Mum that Peter and I were leaving Fiji and flying to Brisbane, as he had been offered work on an Australian newspaper. My big news was that we were engaged and would be getting married — nothing big, most likely in a registry office.

I could detect the concern in Mum's voice. 'Are you sure about this? You haven't known him very long . . . why not come home first?'

Coming home wasn't an option, because I knew as soon as I did, I would spiral into thinking about my son every day. By staying away, I could be totally immersed in this high-octane lifestyle, which involved a lot of risk-taking and setting my own course.

I couldn't tell Mum this.

But now that I was leaving the *Cutty Sark*, and going ashore, maybe — just maybe — I would stop running.

TALES FROM THE BOOKSHOPS: STRANGER THAN FICTION

—

INGER HAS LIVED in Manapōuri all her life. Her family have owned the Manapōuri Hotel and the camping ground for many years, so together with her three brothers she has watched our small town grow.

Years ago, in one of the many sheds on the property of the camping ground, she found some boxes of old books that used to be in the Manapōuri community library. She drove up to my bookshops and, with the hugest smile, dropped off a truly unusual collection, including a novel by Frank G. Slaughter with a very raunchy cover showing a couple passionately embracing, with very few clothes on. Inger had picked it out especially because the title was *The Song of Ruth*, which she found hilarious!

But what *is* an interesting coincidence is that some years earlier a friend of ours from the UK, Jeff Gulvin, writing as Adam Armstrong, had published a book called *Song of the Sound*, set in Fiordland and the subantarctic, and it actually was a little bit about me, but mostly about Lance.

Lance, under the name of John-Cody Gibbs, is the main character, together with our charter boat, *Breaksea Girl*. The tagline for the book reads: 'An unforgettable story of love and adventure set in one of the world's last unspoiled wildernesses.' In the book my name is Mahina, and sadly, Mahina gets short shrift — she is disposed of early in the book so that her rugged husband, John/Lance, can have a passionate relationship with a young woman who has come to Fiordland to study dolphins.

Jeff came over from England and lived with us as he wrote the book, staying in the small self-contained flat attached to our home. One morning he came in to see me and said, 'Hi Ruthie. Thought I should tell you that Mahina will have to die early on in the book. Sorry about this.'

'*What*?! You're going to kill me off? How is Lance, or should I say John-Cody, going to feel about this?'

'Oh, he'll be fine. He finds a new love.'

'Well, that's nice — lucky him!'

This book became a bestseller in the Netherlands and other parts of Europe in 2003. That was when we had our first bookshop, 45 South and Below, and I sold over 50 copies of *Song of the Sound*. I would often turn up at our office and people would be waiting for me, clinging to their copy of the book, smiling enthusiastically as I arrived. All were devoted fans of Adam Armstrong. They wanted to see where he slept, where he wrote the book; they wanted to walk around our back yard (which is mentioned) — and check out the bathroom (also mentioned!).

We were even visited by a film director who was keen to make a movie based on the book and intended to film it in Manapōuri, on board *Breaksea Girl* and in our house! I said no to the latter, as we cherished what little privacy we had left. Thankfully (for us), they didn't get the funding so the whole thing died.

CHAPTER 10

MY BRIEF CAREER AS A BURGLAR

Within three months of our wedding at sea I was pregnant. Peter and I still had not been officially married; it didn't seem important. We had had the kind of wedding that mattered to us — who cared if we didn't have the paperwork?

Strange as it seems looking back, I never told my family I was pregnant. As much as I tried to shake it, I had an inner fear that something would go wrong. I wanted to wait until after the baby was born and was safe and healthy before I told my family. Mum and Dad had been through enough dramas when it came to my life — I felt like I could only offer them good news.

Peter and I were settled initially in Brisbane. I was 23 years old, had very little money, and the only clothes I owned were the few I had worn over the past year sailing around the Pacific.

We found a small flat just on the southern outskirts of town: cheap, dirty, no furniture, but luckily there was a stove and fridge. The common laundry downstairs was shared with three other flats in the complex. It was coming into summer so at least heating wasn't required. Peter was working as a newspaper reporter so we had just enough income to cover rent, food and power — and make a deposit on an old VW Beetle.

After five days of settling in and cleaning the flat, it was time for me to get a job. Having no suitable clothes for a face-to-face interview, and no spare money to buy any, I hatched a plan to borrow some — 'borrow' perhaps being a bit of a euphemism. The first step of the plan was to walk the streets around us, paying particular attention to the location of the clothesline on each property. It was very, *very* important that I wasn't caught, so I made detailed notes about each property that offered me an opportunity.

At around 2.30 a.m. one night I set out with a small torch in one hand and a pen and paper in my pocket. When I had twelve addresses carefully noted, I returned home and ran through the questionnaire I had devised. Was the clothesline accessible enough to ensure easy access but far enough from a window that I wouldn't be seen? Was it too well-lit or too close to a main path or the road?

Only eight of the twelve addresses passed the test. Next, it was time to work out what kinds of clothes were going to be on offer for me to 'borrow'. I highlighted the eight addresses on a map and planned a walking route that meant I could cover them all in the quickest possible time. Peter was working nights, so I was able to slip out of the flat just after midnight without him knowing. He had no idea what I was up to.

The first four clotheslines on my list failed to deliver anything useful — either they had only men's clothing hung out, or nothing was the right size. Like an adult Goldilocks, I moved on. At address number five I had success, quickly unpegging a pair of stockings, a skirt and a blouse. At address number six I scored a floral-print green dress and a bra.

I hurried home and shut the door behind me, feeling excitement and relief: it had been so easy! I took off my old faded jeans and T-shirt and tried on the dress. It felt wonderful, if a little big, but I had a needle and thread so I could easily take it in temporarily around the waist and neckline. The bra fitted perfectly, as did the stockings.

The next morning I rang around hospitals and aged-care homes requesting work. I got an interview for the next day at a small hospital for the elderly that was within walking distance of the flat. I spilled the beans to Peter and he laughed. 'So I'm living with a burglar now?' I had never stolen before and I really didn't see myself as a burglar. I saw myself as a woman with few choices who was desperate to get work. I promised myself I would return the clothing as soon as possible.

Not only did I get the job — as a night nurse — but I was given two uniforms. The only problem was I was required to wear white walking shoes, and I didn't have any. I was to start in three days' time, giving me enough time to solve the shoe problem.

That night I returned the skirt and blouse to address number five. In the skirt pocket I placed a note: 'I am sorry to have borrowed your clothing but I needed something nice to wear to a job interview. I have to keep the stockings, but will buy you a new pair when I get my first pay.'

At address number six I pegged the green dress back up on the line, having unstitched my sewing. As it had no pockets, I pegged a note next to the dress, saying I would replace the bra with a new one when I received my first wages.

The shoe problem was solved when Peter gave me $5. There were a number of op shops in the area and I found a pair of well-worn white shoes that fitted perfectly.

As promised, on my first pay day I replaced the bra and the stockings, pegging them to the clotheslines with a thank-you note. Although the whole 'burglary' had gone smoothly, I was pleased it was all over. The excitement of plotting, the anticipation of actually pulling off the plan and the stress of being caught were all now behind me. Job done!

———

AFTER THREE WEEKS on night duty, my shift was changed to afternoons. Now instead of just monitoring the residents during the night, which included taking them to the toilet, changing wet beds, administering medication and keeping their fluids up, I had the opportunity to chat and interact with them on a more personal level. My shift started at 2 p.m., at the same time as visiting hours. And this is when I confronted the consequences of my brief career as a burglar.

A young woman who visited often came down the corridor towards Mr Lamb's private room. She stepped lightly as though she had been told to be quiet. Her short blonde hair was cut in a fashionable bob and her smart yellow sandals perfectly matched her dress. I was coming out of Mr Lamb's room when I saw her approaching.

'Oh my God!' I gasped. I recognised the dress. After taking a breath, I realised the colour was different — the woman's dress was blue, not green. The cut was exactly the same — the fitted waist, flared skirt, sleeveless style in bright colours was replacing the miniskirt and hotpants that had swept the Western world during the 1960s.

'Hi, Ruth. How's Grandad today?' the woman asked.

'Cheeky as usual. He is all ready for visitors.' After a short hesitation I added, 'Lovely dress — where did you get it?'

'At that little shopping centre in Wardell Street — the shop next to the hairdressers.'

'Oh, I know that shop, I live nearby. Oh well, must get on, lots to do.' My heart was still racing as I rushed for cover in a nearby room.

Pay day came around and with the budget now well under control, I walked up to the Wardell Street shops. I had decided to buy a dress from the wee fashion shop. Not just any dress but an exact copy of my burglar dress.

The rack stretched along the wall and there, amazingly, were at least four of the burglar dresses in different colours.

'Can I help you?' asked the attendant.

'Yes, I would like to try on this dress, size 10 in green if possible.'

'This has been a very popular dress. Must be the pretty flowers and wonderful skirt, which sits beautifully over layered petticoats.' She looked along the rack and then sighed. 'Sorry, no green left in size 10; only blue. One lady recently bought two, one green and one blue. Apparently the first dress she bought, the green one, was stolen off her clothesline. Who on earth would have thought that could happen around here? Whoever it was took her bra as well!'

'How incredible,' I mumbled, with an awful sinking feeling. 'I'll try on the blue one, please.'

It fitted perfectly, and even though it was a little more expensive than I had budgeted for, I decided to buy a lovely white lacy petticoat as well.

'The poor woman was so upset,' the attendant chatted on. 'And the *weird* thing is, the day after she'd bought the second dress, the blue one, her green one appeared back on the clothesline! *And* with a letter! Some strange story about the person who stole the dress needing it for a job interview. How's that for a story? Poor lady. Her grandfather has just recently been placed into care; I feel so sorry for her. Now she thinks someone is watching her place and she's scared at night. And of course,' she paused for dramatic effect, 'she is *not* leaving her washing out at night, which is most inconvenient.'

'Why is that?' I asked, trying not to show too much interest.

'She lives alone, works five days a week, visits her grandfather — who has heart trouble — on her days off, and is also looking after her grandmother, who still lives in her own home on the northern side of town.'

I picked up the parcel, smiled at the attendant and, with a heavy feeling of guilt, walked slowly home. To me, it had seemed like a short-term solution, with no damage done. However, the victim of my 'crime' had been left feeling scared and targeted.

Whichever way I thought about it, there was only one thing to be done to settle the whole stupid situation and alleviate this poor woman's stress. But it had to be planned carefully.

———

EDWARD LAMB WAS 89, born in 1881. As a young man he was tall, slim and handsome, as confirmed by the family photos in his room. He was still tall and slim but he walked with a stoop, and his hair was now grey and sparse. What I liked about him was that he was a gentleman who loved to talk, especially about his life growing up in Brisbane. He told me he had joined the Queensland Marine Defence Force at the age of sixteen in 1897, and as I had been a Wren we had a lot in common, both being interested in boats, naval history and the sea.

I was making up his bed the morning after my shopping expedition, as he sat in the armchair by the window. Head down, concentrating on pulling the sheets tightly on the bed, I quietly asked him when his granddaughter was coming to see him again.

'Catherine always comes on Sunday at 1400 hours. You already know that, Ruthie.'

'Yes, sorry, I'm a little nervous today. I need to tell you something I have done that I'm not proud of.'

This was not how I had planned to deal with this; I had decided the right thing to do was to tell Catherine face to face.

'We all have something in our lives we're not proud of,' Edward replied kindly. 'There are many times when I have felt I have let someone down. It's a matter of learning from it. Have you learnt from whatever this is?'

I nodded and then sat on the edge of the bed near his chair. I didn't want to cry but I felt the tears start to gather.

'Come on Ruthie, my girl, what is it?'

Once I started to tell him the story it just gushed out, every detail. On the one hand it was a relief, but I was worried I had destroyed our friendship.

'Dear, oh dear, what a tale,' the old man said gently. 'I think we can clear this up on Sunday with Catherine, don't you?' He gazed at me with soft grey eyes, reached out for my hand and squeezed it, and then, amazingly, he laughed. This made me cry even more.

'Now, here's what we will do,' he said. 'Catherine will arrive at 1400 and then you will come and see us at 1430 when you have your afternoon-tea break. There is one condition: you have to wear your so-called "burglar dress".'

There was a warm but sneaky twinkle in his eyes as he said it.

———

AS I ENTERED Edward's room that Sunday, Catherine looked up and smiled when she saw my dress. 'So you went and bought one — it looks lovely on you.'

I thanked her and sat down. Edward had my cup of tea poured and a small plate with orange cake sat next to it.

Sitting opposite Edward was his friend James, another of my favourite patients. He was Scottish and had practised law for most of his life. He coughed lightly, shuffled in his chair and then said, 'Edward Lamb believes it is his filial duty to strongly support his granddaughter during this very unusual time. It has been brought to our attention that you, Ruth, planned and executed the taking of another person's clothing from their clothesline under cover of darkness. Is this correct?'

I was astonished: they already knew all the details and were now considering judgement! The three of them were looking directly at me.

'Yes,' I whispered.

'And on another night, you replaced the said clothing together with a handwritten note,' said James, passing me the note. 'Is this your handwriting?'

'Can I just say something please?' I asked in a very soft voice.

'Answer my question.'

I looked at the note and confirmed that it was my writing.

James glanced across to Catherine and Edward, 'Shall I call witnesses?'

'What witnesses, Mr McIntyre?' I asked, my voice shaking a little.

Edward shook his head and addressed James. 'No need for witnesses.'

I gulped down some lukewarm tea, as my mouth had gone completely dry. I felt like an idiot sitting there in the same dress as Catherine: it was like a beacon confirming my guilt.

'I am so very sorry, Catherine,' I said. 'I didn't believe I was stealing. I just needed to get work and I had absolutely no clothes for the interview. Please believe me.'

Totally ignoring me, James continued. 'I have discussed this with my clients and we have decided to give you our decision in writing.'

James Thomas McIntyre handed me an official-looking envelope. 'Open it now please and read it aloud.'

I did what I was told.

> *Catherine Lamb, teacher, Edward Lamb, retired naval officer, and James Thomas McIntyre, retired solicitor, hereby find Ruth not guilty and award her with the attached document.*

I turned the page to look at the attached document. It was a cheque made out in my name for the exact cost of my burglar dress and petticoat. I burst out crying, and then laughing, as Catherine came over to give me a big hug. Edward rang his call bell and gave me a wink.

At this point the nursing sister came to his door and

asked what he wanted. 'Oh, Sister! As you can see, my granddaughter is having trouble trying to decide which colour dress to buy so we have asked Ruthie here to help us decide. She'll be another fifteen minutes on her break if that is all right with you.' He gave her a huge smile and there was no way she could say no. I ate the orange cake, drank a fresh cup of tea and realised that Edward had played a brilliant hand. Better than any I could have planned. My short career as a burglar had ended in a very satisfactory manner.

TALES FROM
THE BOOKSHOPS:
FAMILY HEIRLOOMS

———

I HAVE TO be very careful what books I buy in, as shelf space is so limited in my wee shop. I rely on people bringing in books to sell: they might be downsizing, or family members have moved out — or the books might be part of a deceased estate.

I have a strict code when it comes to estates: I will not buy books until the person has been deceased for at least six months. I make sure I ask whether the rest of the family have been given the opportunity to keep any books themselves, and I discuss with them the importance of keeping the books in the family. It's surprisingly common, when someone in the family dies, for all of their books to be quickly boxed up and dropped off at a charity shop, or taken to a book dealer, with no one realising that some of them are rare and worth a lot of money.

I don't give people an overall price for a box of books; I price each book individually, which can take many hours. If I am invited to go into a home to price a library and identify rare or special books, I explain that even if they don't want to keep the books for themselves, maybe a grandchild will treasure them later in life. Every book has a story, and many carry precious memories.

When I hold one of my mother's books I remember her; I touch the same page she touched, I read the same words she read. Books collected over many years become part of the family. They have been loved, read and re-read, and have often travelled around the world. They live in silence for years in a family home bearing witness to many special occasions, bringing the reader joy and sometimes tears.

I therefore handle every book with care. I go through the pages looking for handwritten notes in the margins, or wee drawings of insects, leaves and flowers. Often I find letters, pressed flowers, postcards and photographs, and in one botany book I found a letter written on a leaf.

Alan Petrie, retired, from Te Anau, brought me some books he wanted to sell. The leaf in question was tucked neatly inside one of the books, still in perfect condition, pale green and supple. Written on it was this text:

Hello! Writing this postcard from Preservation Inlet where we just saw two whales; watched them for about half an hour close to the ship. Great trip so far; weather not the best but cannot do much about that. Will see you sometime in the afternoon on Sunday.

Love William.

Māori used the large, pliable leaves of rangiora (*Brachyglottis repanda*) for wrapping food and swaddling babies, and as a poultice for wounds. Later, European settlers used it as notepaper and toilet paper, leading to its other common name: 'bushman's friend'. The related *Brachyglottis rotundifolia* (muttonbird scrub), which is found only in coastal areas in the lower South Island and Stewart Island, has smaller but thicker leaves that were sometimes used as postcards. People (especially tourists) wrote on the leaves, placed a stamp in the corner, and posted them from Paterson Inlet post office on Stewart Island to addresses all over New Zealand and overseas.

The New Zealand Post Office did not share the public's enthusiasm for these souvenirs. In 1906 the NZPO advised that 'the transmission of tree-leaves posted loose and bearing written communications to the United Kingdom or to countries in transit through the United Kingdom is forbidden'. In 1912 the ban was extended to include 'any address'. Finally, in 1915 the advice was: 'Loose tree-leaves are prohibited, and if posted, are to be sent to the Dead Letter Office for disposal.'

I rang Alan and told him of my find. It turned out that the letter was from his son, and obviously never posted. I was very happy to return the book and the leaf postcard to his father. Alan told William the leaf had been found, and I received a wonderful email from Sheila, his mother: 'Thanks Ruth, William is tickled pink!'

Recently I bought a book from the hospice shop: *A Field Guide to the Birds of New Zealand*, by Falla, Sibson and

Turbott. It was a 1972 reprint of the 1966 publication, in fair to good condition. As I flicked through the pages I found a scrap of paper with a letter written in pencil:

> *Hello Luke, I am writing to apolize [sic] for not showing up to help out on the 2nd. Ali only gets Fridays off and we are going to hike the Tongariro Crossing together. May the winds be kind to you! I hope this book is useful, just return it to Ali whenever you like. Thanks for your hospitality on the boat last night.*
>
> *Vera.*

I placed the note back in the book, where it had been for so many years; it will stay with the book when it is sold. Whenever I find such treasures I try to imagine who the people were, and where they were when they wrote the note. Who were Vera and Ali? Did they successfully hike the Tongariro Crossing? Wouldn't it be incredible if they read *this* book and realise their note has survived all this time . . .

TRAGEDY RETURNS

As a journalist, Peter was spending more and more time away travelling around Australia, researching stories. In mid-1970 he took an assignment that involved making his way to the Northern Territory for two weeks.

I was sound asleep one night in our flat when the stillness of the night was broken by a loud knock on the door. The police were standing on my doorstep. A policewoman placed an arm around my shoulders and guided me towards a chair. After a few questions to confirm who I was, she told me why they were there. 'We have just been notified that your husband has been killed.'

I didn't believe her. I only heard parts of the conversation as they carefully explained the details of the car accident. With genuine concern, they sat with me and talked, making numerous cups of tea before arranging for a friend to come over and stay with me. I sat stiffly on the edge of my chair. No tears, no emotion, no sign that I had even heard them.

———

PETER'S PARENTS CLAIMED his body, making it very clear they wanted nothing to do with me as I was a Catholic and they were Protestant. They didn't recognise my position as Peter's partner and they certainly didn't recognise our marriage.

The only remaining piece of our relationship I had left was my pregnancy; I desperately wanted a little boy.

Depression clawed its way into my life. I couldn't work, I couldn't sleep. I was anaemic — a walking shell. Still I didn't call home; I couldn't bear to tell my parents any of this. One night, when things got really bad, I called Lifeline. Doug Kerr, a lawyer involved with the helpline, arranged for me to move in with his family, and within a couple of days I was surrounded by love. I felt safe. Liz, his amazing wife, already had four young girls and was pregnant again. Without the immediate support of this family, I cannot imagine what would have happened to me.

Going into labour, experiencing the physical reality of giving life to a child, pierced my depressive fog — not just with pain, but also relief. No one could take this precious moment away from me: I had given birth to the son I had so hoped for.

As the doctor placed him on my body I touched his head, feeling the warm dampness. His tiny fingers curled around mine as though he, too, sought our special bond. I gazed in wonder as he moved — pouting his lips, frowning, poking his tongue out.

'Joshua,' I whispered. 'You are Joshua.'

Our happy bubble lasted only a matter of hours. The doctor came to my bedside and Liz was with him, looking concerned. She held my hand as the doctor explained that Joshua had Rh (rhesus) disease. During the pregnancy the mother's Rh-negative antibodies enter the placenta and fight the baby's Rh-positive cells, making the baby sick. Joshua, my second child, was extremely ill and required specialist care. His heart was failing, he needed an urgent blood transfusion and had to be transferred from Southport Hospital on the coast to Brisbane straight away. I could follow the next day when I was stronger.

Liz, a nurse and a priest stood, dull-faced, at the end of my bed as I clung to Joshua, staring at his tiny pale face. I tried to engrave into my mind every detail, every minute feature. The baptism was brief; according to Catholic doctrine he was now 'a child of God'. I looked at the priest with hatred and anger as I lashed out, 'He was a child of God as soon as he was conceived!'

The priest nodded, saying with a tired smile, 'If anything should happen to this little one, he will go straight to heaven. Surely that is what is important.'

'Get out!' I seethed. 'Get out. He is going to live!'

'We must be prepared for whatever God has planned.'

I held Joshua closer. It was as though I was trying to take him back into my womb to hide him, protect him.

There is normally no risk of Rh disease during a first pregnancy; most issues occur during second and subsequent pregnancies. With horror I realised that the Rh factor Joshua had was a result of the rape, because he was my second child. Even my blood was tainted.

My cheek touched his; it was soft and warm. I rocked back and forth, back and forth, my moaning like the soulful cry of the wind. Pain seeped deep into my body.

The nurse came towards me and held out her arms for Joshua. I stared at her, hardly seeing her through my tears, still clinging to my tiny baby. With a sense of determination, she leant forward and gently took him from me.

That was the last time I ever saw Joshua. He died only hours later. I was still in hospital when he was buried and was not allowed to attend the funeral. All I could afford was a small wooden cross in common ground. My only proof of his short life is his death certificate:

Joshua Alexander. 13½ hours old. October 1970.
Royal Women's Hospital.

Cause of death:
(1) Interstitial emphysema, pneumothorax and
pneumomediastinum
— Hyaline membrane disease

(2) Haemolytic disease due to RH sensitisation

———

A FEW BRIEF months of happiness had been swamped by horrendous, life-sapping events.

I doubt if I could survive the events of 1970-72 again, but back then I was young, and maybe the rape and having to give up my son back in 1963 had, in some way, prepared me for these latest blows.

The Ruth I projected to everyone was only skin deep; the inner Ruth was in complete turmoil. And yet my survival instincts kicked in again; like a wild animal, I was preparing to turn and run as fast as I could. I was still in shock, from Peter's death, and now Joshua's, but I knew I needed to get away, as far away from the nightmare as possible. An offer of work in Papua New Guinea a month later prompted the move.

Before I left, I went to Joshua's grave site and planted a miniature rose bush in front of the white wooden cross. The tiny red roses bravely displayed their colour in their new surroundings of death and sadness.

I turned to leave, vowing never to return.

CHAPTER 12

ARRIVING
IN RABAUL

My mother and father were not thrilled when I rang
and told them I was going to New Guinea. Dad told
me I could be eaten and they would never see me again.
I told him he was reading the wrong books.

I arrived in Rabaul on 25 June 1971.

Rabaul lies on the eastern end of the island of New
Britain. It became the provincial capital of the Australian-
mandated Territory of New Guinea in 1914 when it
was taken from the Germans. Situated on the Simpson
Harbour, which is sheltered by the Gazelle Peninsula,
it was considered one of the safest harbours in the
South Pacific. During the Second World War it became

strategically significant because of its proximity to the Japanese territory of the Caroline Islands, then a site of a major Japanese naval base. We frequently explored the many abandoned tunnels, war rooms and sleeping areas, where abandoned equipment, aircraft, landing barges and weapons could still be found.

Despite its dramatic history, this large, sheltered harbour ensured that after the war Rabaul once again became an important South Pacific port.

We all learnt to speak pidgin English, and the more I came to understand the social system in PNG, the more embarrassed I became. A lot of the expatriates — 'expats', as we were called — treated their servants with disdain to the point of cruelty. I quickly realised that many of the expats were pompous drunks living a life of colonial self-importance, mistreating their house boys and girls and often keeping a native mistress or two.

Rabaul was socially and racially stratified, and even within the colonial community there were hierarchies and exclusions. It was considered to be just another part of Australia so they believed they had complete control over everything. Most of the infrastructure, including the Commonwealth Bank, the ANZ Bank and Telecom, had been built by the Australians. We used Australian money, we stood and sang 'God Save the Queen' when we went to the movies, and we all had servants. These people would not have survived if they had returned to Australia or New

Zealand as their façade of a lifestyle would have ended very abruptly.

The job I had been offered was a six-month stint at the Ascot Hotel as a chef. The Ascot had a contract with Ansett Airlines to provide in-flight breakfasts for the early-morning flight to Port Moresby. We also prepared meals for the air traffic controllers and other residents of the single men's quarters, so my days started very early and finished late, with a short break during the day.

One of the single guys who was known to be a bookie came in for meals. He rented premises in the Chinese sector of Rabaul for illegal betting on horse racing. When he heard that I played cards he was very eager for me to join his 'team'. I had nothing better to do so I agreed, and he taught me the art of 'pencilling'.

A bookie's penciller keeps a running total of the money the book is holding on all the horses. I wrote the betting tickets; kept track of all the bets being placed; kept the blackboards up to date, recording changes to the field if a horse was scratched; and reported on track conditions. Everything revolved around the patchy radio reception, and the many phone calls from bookies around Australia. It was always exceptionally noisy, busy and exciting — and totally illegal. The chaos suited me: I grew to love New Guinea, the work, the local Tolai people and the social life. Slowly, I was starting to rebuild my life.

Rabaul is situated on an active volcanic system and

Mt Tavurvur, on the south-east of the town, is an active stratovolcano. We had learnt to live with the smell of Rabaul, which was like nowhere else — sulphur combined with betel nut and topped off with the ever-present fragrance of the frangipani flower. Small earthquakes were part of daily life; we just grew used to them. However, a month after my arrival there was a big one. On 27 July 1971 a quake measuring a massive 8.3 on the Richter scale caused widespread damage throughout the islands, as well as multiple tidal waves. It was one of the most severe earthquakes in the history of Papua New Guinea.

We were immediately evacuated to high ground above the township. From there we watched the enormous tsunamis sweep into the township, flooding the Travel-odge and the entire main shopping area, sucking cars and boats back out to sea. The small island in the middle of the harbour was completely washed away, and incredibly, we briefly saw shipwrecks on the sea floor.

(Much later, in 1994, Tavurvur erupted, along with Vulcan, another active volcano on the western side of the harbour. Rabaul was completely destroyed.)

At the time I was there, the Australian government was facing an increasingly well-organised push for self-government. The Gazelle local council had been exclusively Papua New Guinean, but after some deliberation and consultation it was proclaimed multi-racial, against the wishes of many locals. The Tolai-organised Mataungan

Association began a campaign of dissent, refusing to pay taxes until the council went back to having exclusively PNG membership. Violence erupted and there were arrests.

We had just recovered from the massive earthquake when, on 19 August 1971, Jack Emanuel, the Australian District Commissioner and leader of the colonial administration in the Rabaul District, was murdered. He had served the region for many years, he spoke Kuanua, and was regarded as having a special place in the Tolai community. A group of ten village leaders wearing traditional face and hair decoration had confronted Emanuel and the police when he was called in to try and mediate a land dispute. The local paper reported that one of the men spoke briefly with Emanuel before they all turned and went into the bush.

Sometime later, when Emanuel had not returned, a small party of police went down the bush path to look for him. They found his body: he had been stabbed to death with an old Japanese wartime bayonet. Some accused Mataungan Association members, but their involvement has never been proven.

I remember the day it happened: police in protective gear all over the town, being told to stay inside with doors locked unless employed in essential work. We didn't know who to trust, even among the locals we worked with.

As the country began preparing for the possibility of self-government, part of my work was training local girls to prepare the breakfasts and cook main meals for the single men. Political turmoil was rife, but I had a job to do. Against this backdrop I met dark-haired, gentle Matt, an Australian air traffic controller in PNG on a three-year contract. He was shy and quiet, with a kind smile and soft brown eyes. Although we were different in so many ways, we started to date.

I warned him that a relationship with me would not be easy, and that I was an emotional mess, but he fell in love anyway. He was easy to be with, he made me laugh, and he gave me back the confidence to believe my chaotic life could change. He was everything I needed and yearned for — I was falling in love with him too.

My temporary visa was due to expire. Matt wanted me to stay — I'd been offered more work and there was really no reason for me to leave but I knew I was back on the run. I didn't have the confidence to settle down as I considered myself to be a bad deal when it came to relationships. Everything I touched seemed to fall apart, and further pain down the line felt to me inevitable. I couldn't face the prospect.

In many ways I didn't want to leave, but when a small 30-foot (9-metre) sloop named *Islander* sailed into the harbour I had no hesitation in signing up as crew. Mike, the boat's owner, had solo sailed from Madang to Rabaul but wanted a hand as he headed up through northern Papua New Guinea and on to West Irian and Java.

I set one condition clearly up front: I would not be his sleeping partner. 'You are bloody lucky to have me as crew,' I told him, 'so don't stuff it up. I will not hesitate to get off and leave you, no matter where we are.' Mike promised, and was true to his word. We became an extremely compatible team and good friends.

I told Matt that I would come back once we reached Singapore. He accepted that I had to go and said he would wait for me. Only now do I realise what incredible insight and understanding he had. He let me go, even though it broke his heart.

TALES FROM
THE BOOKSHOPS:
HORSES FOR COURSES

———

IT WAS SATURDAY and both Wee Bookshops were busy. People were sitting outside browsing through books, children sat out in the sun reading, a dog was tied up to the trailer near the bucket of water, and a baby lay asleep in a pram.

The Australian couple came straight up to me. 'Don't suppose you have any books on horse racing? Really small bookshop, so, stupid question.'

I knew I didn't have any books on horse racing in the shop, but I did have one in my own library, on a horse called Fine Cotton. Since my stint as a penciller for a bookie in Rabaul I had retained a small interest in horse racing. I was interested in this particular horse and the associated scam because I was working in Kings Cross when it went down in 1984, and I had heard of some of the people involved.

Fine Cotton was owned by a syndicate headed by John Gillespie. They bought another horse that looked almost identical to Fine Cotton but was a much better racer.

Unfortunately for the syndicate, the new horse, Dashing

Solitaire, was injured and unable to race when the planned ring-in was due to take place. Having already invested so much money, they cast about to find another horse. With time running out they settled on an open-class horse several grades above Fine Cotton.

There was just one problem: the horses were different colours. Fine Cotton was an eight-year-old brown gelding with white markings on his hind legs, whereas Bold Personality was a seven-year-old bay gelding with no markings.

Easy. Syndicate members bought a few bottles of Clairol hair colouring and did their best. On race day, having forgotten the peroxide to whiten some leg patches on Bold Personality, they reached for some white paint to do the job.

If the scam had succeeded, the syndicate would have collected over one million dollars. But it failed dismally, and six individuals were banned from the racing fraternity for life. John Gillespie and trainer Hayden Haitana served jail terms.

I showed the book to the Australian collector, who was delighted and amazed. He had hundreds of books in his collection, but he didn't have this one.

'This is very exciting — I'm so glad I stopped by. How much?'

I knew that I could have asked whatever I liked and he would have paid, but I also knew the book was going to a good home.

'How about ten dollars?'

'Done, little lady — a real bargain!'

CHAPTER 13

PLEASE WORRY

Once again, I kept a diary over the months I sailed on *Islander*, but this was lost when *Crusader*, another yacht I sailed on years later, was sunk in the Bay of Bengal, with the loss of all crew. I had had major concerns about the abilities of the skipper/owner and had the sense to get off *Crusader* a few months earlier.

Thankfully, my father had kept some of my letters. My parents followed my 'adventures and misadventures' through my letters. As a mother myself, I can only now understand how constantly they must have worried about me. Some of my letters took over a month to get to New Zealand; many never arrived. Just before I left New Zealand my sister had married Colin, a builder — a steady, honest man. At least one of us had a chaos-free life.

I was distraught when we sailed out of Rabaul, torn between wanting to stay and the urgency I felt to leave before I sabotaged yet another relationship.

16th Sept 1971

Dear Mum and Dad, Jill and Colin, Aunty etc,

Excuse the writing and the spots of salt water all over the paper but I am writing this at sea. We finally left Rabaul 6:30 12th Sept; we sailed all day and anchored that night at a tiny village ...

At the end of this letter I wrote:

Well I must go, please worry, I am fine,
Love from Ruth xxxx

I had missed out the crucial word 'don't'. I can laugh now, but what did Mum think when she read my instruction to 'please worry'?!

Another adventure had begun. We settled into an easy routine on board, standing watches for as long as we wanted, eating when hungry, and I slowly felt the solitude and calm seep into the depths of my being. The *Islander* was small, with almost no head room. There was a two-burner gimballed stove (which tilts to remain level even when the boat is not), a chart table that was used for multiple tasks, two narrow bunks, a tiny toilet, and a sail locker up near the anchor chain and ropes. Access to the engine was gained by lifting the cockpit floorboards, not the easiest of operations to carry out at sea.

From Wewak we sailed on to Vanimo, the small capital of the West Sepik province of PNG and also the country's north-westernmost harbour, only 22 kilometres from the border of Indonesia. At that time there were only 180 Europeans living there, together with over 1000 military at a Royal Pacific Islands Regiment army camp, guarding the border against the constant stream of Papuan refugees attempting to cross from West Irian.

In 1971 very few yachts had sailed from Papua New Guinea to West Irian. The Indonesian government had only just opened the border — under strict controls that created a problem for us. It turned out that our charts were incorrect, as the names of the harbours and ports had been changed since the area had been taken over from the Dutch.

On our arrival at Vanimo customs officers came on board and searched the boat thoroughly. At the end of the inspection one of them said, 'You are now one bottle of whisky short — this one is mine.' We weren't about to object. Six armed Indonesian soldiers were stationed on the wharf, rifles over their backs and batons in their belts. We had a loaded .22 well hidden under Mike's bunk but they didn't find it.

The customs officers escorted us to the Immigration Department to fill out the necessary forms to sail through West Irian. From there the armed escort marched us to the Quarantine Department, where more forms were filled out, and finally to the Navy Department. The township was sparse: only a few Papuans were about. We went to the market but decided not to buy anything as a lot of the food was rotten. Over half a million Indonesians lived in Vanimo, and the military presence was everywhere. We met two United Nations workers at the market who told us not to drink the water or refill our water tank in West Irian (now West Papua) as it was full of mosquito larvae and cholera bacteria. They also told us to move on as quickly as possible as it was dangerous, with bribery and theft rampant.

After exchanging money and gathering all the required paperwork, we departed for Jayapura, a poor town riddled with cholera and malaria, and with no mail system. The only way to get letters home was through the United Nations, which flew its own planes in and out. Mum told me later that many of my letters never arrived and some of them had had the stamps removed. 'Please worry' had turned out to be a prescient, although accidental, warning.

While we were in Jayapura, we had a visit from the wives

of the Indonesian high commissioner and a high-ranking naval official. They wanted to look through *Islander*, and arrived dressed in beautiful embroidered jackets, matching trousers, dainty sandals and lots of jewellery, their hair and makeup immaculate. It was obviously a grand occasion for them. The steps down from the wharf to our 8-foot (2.4-metre) dinghy were steep and slippery so I took great care explaining to their English-speaking armed guard how they should step aboard. With our first guest seated safely, I turned back and was horrified to see that her companion had decided to *jump* from the wharf into the dinghy.

There was absolutely nothing I could do. The dinghy capsized instantly and the three of us were splashing around in the filthy water. The armed guards were jumping up and down on shore, yelling and pointing their guns at me. I can't remember how I managed to get the two women back onto the wharf; I just recall hanging one of them over the side of the dinghy while I swam with the other one to the steps. Once they were both safely ashore I rowed back out to the boat on my own, shaking with uncontrollable nervous laughter.

The high commissioner was furious. He came storming down to the wharf claiming that I had tried to drown his wife and her companion. Mike and I were standing on the deck of *Islander*, quietly panicking. 'Shit,' said Mike, 'if we get out of this bloody mess we'll be lucky!' And we were — a UN interpreter eventually intervened to defuse the situation. The high commissioner apologised and gave us a peace offering: two cartons of terrible cigarettes and a half-dozen cans of incredibly bad beer, all of which was thrown over the side once we were at sea and out of sight.

An English plantation manager employed by the United Nations in Jayapura had asked us if we would take him across to Manokwari, much further along the coast, where he lived. With no reliable local sea transport he had few opportunities to get there. We were happy to have Peter Foster join us — even though it meant hot bunking — as he spoke numerous languages, which came in extremely handy over the next leg.

Severe weather just off Biak blew us well off course. After fighting gale-force winds and high seas all night, we were relieved to see Numfoor, a small island off the coast of Manokwari, which offered shelter. During the Second World War the Japanese had built an air base there, with three airfields.

As we got closer to the tiny island and set the anchor, canoes appeared out of nowhere and surrounded us. Upon looking closely, we noticed some of the men had human skulls tied around their waists — quite the welcoming party! Mike was once more reduced to panicked whispers but Peter, our multilingual passenger, spoke the local dialect, so managed to get us some fresh food and water.

The locals invited us ashore but Peter quietly advised that we shouldn't accept that seemingly kind offer as this tribe was known to be still practising headhunting. '*What?*' Mike stammered. 'You're bloody joking! This is the 1970s, not the 1870s!' Peter mused that he wasn't sure if the tribe still practised cannibalism, but he knew the heads of Indonesian military were highly prized.

Needless to say, we stayed on the boat, very grateful indeed for Peter's company.

———

WE WERE GREETED in Manokwari by UN staff who supplied us with food, including very welcome coffee and sugar, and also fuel. They were happy to post our mail for us. We told them about our encounter on Numfoor and they confirmed that headhunting was still taking place, with raids regularly carried out on Indonesian troops. An enemy's head was considered a prestigious trophy back in their villages.

In the letter I wrote home before leaving West Irian/ Papua I wrote: 'Well, Dad, I have proven one thing you said was true — there were cannibals here!' (My poor parents . . .)

We farewelled and thanked Peter and set sail for Sorong, our last port before heading away from the equator down through the Ceram Sea to Ambon and across to Java, stopping off at many of the small islands, including Bali, until we arrived at Surabaya. It was in this region that the authorities warned us that, only weeks prior, an American yacht had been attacked and sunk by pirates. The crew survived; they had been allowed to leave the vessel in their life-raft and were picked up by a local fishing boat. It was disconcerting news, particularly after our encounter with the headhunting tribe. This was the start of increasing incidences of piracy around Indonesia, which came to be seen as one of the most dangerous shipping routes.

For safety, we decided to keep close to the Java coast as we headed towards Jakarta. Sailing conditions were perfect so we headed just north of Bawean Island, intending to sail directly to Jakarta with the favourable wind. I was up on the foredeck when Mike yelled from the helm, 'Drop the main!' I assumed I had misunderstood him — there seemed no reason to drop the main, which quickly slows the boat down. Then the main went slack as Mike brought *Islander* into the wind. The jib dropped to the deck. Now there was urgency in his voice: 'Drop the fucking main, Ruth!'

By the time I had released the main halyard I noticed that a 20-foot (6-metre) plywood boat, powered by an outboard, had pulled up alongside us, with four men on board. All of them were armed — three with automatic rifles, and the fourth standing behind a mounted weapon that looked, to my relatively untrained eye, like a bazooka. Our so-called safe route hadn't worked: pirates had found us.

After we had been warned by the authorities, Mike and I had agreed that if we were to strike pirates, we would welcome them on board, stay friendly and, above all, keep smiling. We had hidden our passports, money and important papers, just in case.

'Shit, Ruth, keep fucking smiling!' Mike said through gritted teeth. 'Help the guy come on board!' His face wore a pained grimace. He attached their rope to our starboard side as I helped one of the men come on board. 'Selamat datang, selamet datang,' I repeated over and over, welcoming him on board. That was about the only Indonesian I knew, so I just kept repeating it until Mike told me to shut up.

Mike offered our 'guests' a bottle of whisky; they smiled and accepted it, drinking straight from the bottle. Two men came on board and started to go through the boat, taking what they wanted: clothing, ropes, food, bedding, the last of Mike's whisky, our storm sail, a container of fuel, even a cooking pot and a bucket. We just sat in the cockpit and watched, not moving a muscle, as the other two men had their guns aimed at us. After they had loaded everything into their small runabout they shook our hands politely and thanked us. I went below to get my camera, which was miraculously still sitting behind the chart table. Using gestures, I asked them if I could take a photo.

'Jesus, Ruth — just let them go!' Mike seethed. Then he noticed the four of them posing for me, pointing their guns away from us. One of them even smiled for the camera. I quickly took a photo.

'Terima kasih, thank you,' I called to them. And with that they started their outboard, waved and raced away, heading north.

'Don't you see?' I said to Mike. 'We now have a photo of them that we can take to the authorities!'

We checked the boat over. We were okay, still alive, with enough food to get us to Jakarta. We had sails, our charts, a fixed compass, money and passports. Mike mourned the alcohol — 'Fuck, no whisky!' — but we knew we had been very lucky.

We sailed into the extremely busy port of Jakarta, surrounded by large cargo ships from all over the world, finally anchoring outside the yacht club. *Islander* was the only yacht there, but we were welcomed by the American skipper of a 97-tonne motorboat. He offered us a hot shower and a meal, which was surreal after what we had been through.

When we returned to *Islander* we found we had been robbed — again. We had naively thought we would be safe anchored outside the yacht club. All Mike's clothes were gone; some of my clothes had been taken, including my underwear; plus we'd lost our binoculars, tape recorder, remaining cutlery and the last tank of fuel, which the pirates had generously left for us. Thankfully they hadn't found our passports, papers, cameras or money.

The next day I went in to town to get my film developed so I could report both the piracy and the robbery. My photo of the pirates was reasonably good; not clear enough to identify the men involved but maybe the guns and boat. The police listened, but they were clearly uninterested. I showed them on a map exactly where the pirates had held us up. 'Here, it was right here, in broad daylight!'

One policeman sighed and placed his finger on the map. 'And from there they can go to Malaysia, Sulawesi, and hide on one of the hundreds of islands along our coastline,' he said. 'Where would you like us to start looking?' He gazed at me, waiting for an answer.

'They headed north when they left us.'

'Straight to a proa to unload, get payment and disappear until the next easy target appears.'

We had seen these 'proas' — small outrigger boats — frequently after leaving West Irian/Papua, some with sails, others with outboards. The few that had approached us appeared to be friendly. I felt stupid, realising that nothing could be done. It was a well-organised operation.

'Well, what about our boat being robbed right outside the yacht club?' I said.

Again, they couldn't have been less interested. 'We have five million people here!' one officer shrugged. 'Consider yourself lucky you still have a boat.' He handed me my passport and the photo of the pirates; then, with a show of frustration, he waved me out the door.

———

ON 1 DECEMBER 1971 we finally arrived in Singapore — busy, and safe! After clearing customs and immigration I rushed ashore to ring home, as I hadn't received any mail for six weeks. Mum told me she had been sick but was getting better. I had no idea that in fact she had been diagnosed with cancer.

I collected a pile of mail from the post office, including a letter from Matt in Rabaul telling me there was plenty of work for me there, and he was waiting for me to get back so we could be married. I rang him and explained that we had organised to slip the boat so it could be repaired. I had to find work as I had no money and no, I would not let him pay for my airfares. I was stalling my return to Papua New Guinea.

After slipping *Islander*, Mike returned to Australia to work for three months. I had been offered work in Singapore with an escort agency, which paid exceptionally well. Bronwyn, a tall, big-busted Australian girl, was from another yacht anchored outside the Changi Sailing Club. She explained to me that the agency she worked for needed more European girls.

'Do I have to have sex with the guys?'

'Entirely up to you. You can just be their partner for the evening, have dinner, dance and come home. But if you do have sex with them, you will make masses of money. It's not so bad, really, Ruth. Easy money!'

The companionship part sounded okay and I really was broke, so I signed up. When the woman in charge commented that I was 'small, no titties, no nice clothes, maybe no good!' I didn't argue. Bronwyn organised some dresses for me, which felt very strange after months of living in T-shirts and shorts.

My first outing was a joint date with Bronwyn and two Chinese businessmen. We were picked up by taxi and taken to a hotel. I was extremely nervous and Bronwyn kept saying, 'Just think of the money!'

They took us out to dinner, and thankfully they both spoke English so we managed to hold a conversation. Bronwyn was openly flirting with the older of the two men — 'He'll have more money,' she told me under her breath.

Then the men wanted to dance. Bronwyn's man had his head tucked in her fantastic cleavage, his hips grinding into hers as they shuffled slowly around the floor. As for me, I held my partner at arm's length. He was a little taller than me, had bad breath, oily hair and about ten hands.

'You sleep with me?' he asked.

'No.'

'How much you want to sleep with me?'

'Nothing!'

'Ah, so cheap!' he laughed. I realised he had misunderstood me.

'I mean I'm not going to sleep with you!'

'I pay you in diamonds, maybe that will change your mind,' he grinned.

I pulled away from him, grabbed Bronwyn's arm and marched her off the floor.

'I want to leave; I can't do this,' I told her.

She calmly gave me a card to give to the taxi driver, told me where she was staying and that she would see me in the morning.

I was relieved that the agency paid for the taxi, and I was soon back on board *Islander*. I peeled off the revolting new clothes, climbed back into shorts and T-shirt and sat on deck watching the bright lights of the Singapore skyline.

The next day I received a payment from the agency and was told I wasn't needed any more. 'Told you, you no good!' the woman said sharply, throwing my money onto the desk. It was good money, meaning the pressure was off for a few days, but my very short career as an escort had ended.

TALES FROM THE BOOKSHOPS: LEX, THE BOOKSHOP ASSISTANT

——

LEX, AGED SIX, is a frequent visitor to my bookshop. His younger brother Joe trails behind him sometimes, and his baby sister Flossy visits with Mum. His parents, Sara and Dean, own a holiday home just three houses down the road.

Lex had decided he wanted to become a Bookshop Assistant. In fact he told me that I could 'own' the bigger bookshop and he could 'own' the Children's Bookshop, because I obviously needed help.

After helping me set up the tables and bookshelves outside, Lex positioned his small wooden chair near the door of his bookshop, from where he could observe what was going on in my bookshop.

On his first day at work, after a very short time, he came over to inform me that he would need a desk and computer like mine.

'There is no room in the Children's Bookshop for a desk, Lex,' I replied.

He looked at me very seriously. 'Well, at least a computer. I can use one.'

'What do you think I do on the computer, Lex?'

He answered brightly, 'I don't know, but you can teach me!'

By now we had customers. Lex ran into his bookshop, stationed himself on his chair by the door and closely watched two wee girls as they browsed.

When the girls came across to me to buy two books, Lex followed them.

'I could take their money?' he suggested. 'The books are from my shop.'

I explained that it was probably better if I handled the money, as I needed to take the books off my database.

When we had a break in customers, I asked Lex if he understood money.

'No, but you can teach me.'

'How is your reading, Lex?'

'I can't read many words but I can see the pictures, and Mum and Dad read to me. Mum told me to bring some books home every night.'

'How about you just say hello to everyone and talk to the children in your shop?'

He agreed to this revised job description. He then paced between the two shops waiting for our next customers. When two men arrived, Lex strolled up to them and confidently bellowed, 'Hello!' Then he ran into the Children's Bookshop, taking up his station on the chair.

A young girl came in to drop off three sleepover toys: a pink bunny named Pinky, the camel named Camo and Mornington the cat. Lex proudly took the toys, told her they had to have a bath, then brought them over to me.

Morning two: Lex arrived in a beautiful blue checked shirt, and shoes and socks instead of bare feet. He informed me that it was his uniform. 'You look terrific,' I said. He helped me set up the shops and then I explained why everyone had to 'check in because of Covid'.

'I know! I know! Otherwise they will get sick and I can't go back to school.'

'Exactly. So, from today you will say to customers, "Hello, please check in."'

A couple pulled up, and before they were even out of their car Lex appeared beside them, looked them dead in the eye and declared, 'Hello, please check in.' Then he abruptly turned and raced back to his bookshop with a big smile.

Occasionally, Lex would take a break from his own territory to come and see how things were going in my bookshop. He sidled up to one customer who was browsing a farming book and said, 'I've read that, you know.' When asked what it was about, Lex, who had spotted a photo of a sheep on one page, promptly replied, with great seriousness: 'Sheep.'

Lex worked for an hour and a half each morning when he didn't have things to do at home. He has informed his aunties, uncles, grandfather and sundry other people that he was on wages now, because he was the Bookshop Assistant. When anyone asked him to do any other jobs he would shake his head and say, 'No, Ruth needs me.'

CHAPTER 14

LETTERS
FROM HOME

With Christmas fast approaching, I set myself up as a caretaker for vessels whose owners and crew wanted to go back to the UK, Australia and the US for the festive season. This included organising the slipping of small yachts and preparing them for their next ocean passage, either across the Indian Ocean to Africa or up to the Gulf of Thailand. Mike wanted me back on *Islander* as crew heading across to Africa sometime in the New Year.

But after numerous phone calls from Matt, I decided I would return to Rabaul and get married. I was determined to pay my own way, which was not cheap as I had to fly via Australia. Singapore to Melbourne was NZ$385, and then

I had to fly to Brisbane, and on to Port Moresby and Rabaul on a DC-3 for another NZ$475. When I discovered that the first available flight to PNG was not until mid-January, I decided to fill in the time hitchhiking up to Kuala Lumpur and possibly Bangkok. I didn't book any flights, fearful that an unforeseen tragedy might sabotage my opportunity to be happy.

After buying new clothes at the Thieves Market in Singapore, and with savings of over $1500, I packed my sailor's kit bag and then boarded the overnight train to KL, where I stayed in a youth hostel for 33 cents a night.

I then started to hitchhike to Bangkok, and was quickly picked up by a Malaysian businessman in a Mercedes. How fabulous was that! The Vietnam War was in its twelfth year, and although New Zealand forces were withdrawn in 1970 and 1971, the war didn't end until 1975 when the US, which had backed the Republic of Vietnam in the south, was finally defeated. This was the first war in which New Zealand had not fought alongside our traditional ally, Britain. Instead, our participation reflected New Zealand's increasingly strong defence ties with the US and Australia.

New Zealand's involvement in Vietnam was highly controversial and sparked protests and condemnation at home and abroad. In 1971 some 30,000 people protested all over New Zealand, forcing a re-examination of our foreign policy, and an eventual withdrawal.

I reached Butterworth, an Australian air-force base in

Penang, Malaysia, where a number of American military were stationed for R & R (rest and recreation). It was then that I decided that, since I was in the vicinity, I would try to get into Cambodia, hoping to understand the politics behind the war. I rang home before leaving Butterworth, letting my family know my next stop would be Bangkok, where I would collect my mail and also apply for a visa to enter Cambodia.

Bangkok grew rapidly after the Second World War, as a result of US aid and government investment. During the Vietnam War, thousands of US military visited Pattaya Beach, about 100 kilometres from Bangkok, for R & R. This quickly turned the small fishing village into one of the largest red-light districts in the world. Soldiers sometimes called the breaks 'I & I' (intoxication and intercourse), firmly establishing it as a sex tourism destination. My three-day stay at Pattaya Beach was disturbing; I watched the numerous young men and women working the streets and bars. Drugs were readily available and it was here that I first smoked hash; as a non-smoker I thankfully found it an unpleasant experience.

On arrival in Bangkok I went straight to the post office to collect my mail. On the top of the pile was a telegram from home that had arrived a week earlier:

Your mum extremely sick please come home
Love from Aunty

I rang immediately. Mum had terminal cancer.

I flew out of Singapore five days later. I hadn't been home for over three years.

———

DAD MET ME at Christchurch Airport, wearing his signature cheese-cutter cap, looking pale, his blue eyes red-rimmed. The only luggage I had was my navy kit bag, which he hoisted onto his shoulder easily, hardly a word spoken between us. Mum was his first and only love; they had married very young, melding together perfectly, living for each other. Mum was just 46.

They now lived in Riccarton. Dad was working night shifts at the Crown Lynn pottery so he could be with Mum every day. He was running on autopilot: no whistling, just a quiet, heavy presence.

Mum had always been tiny, full of energy, with dancing eyes and wonderful red hair. She was sitting on the couch waiting for me, and her eyes filled with tears when I came through the door. It was the first day of the four precious months we would share.

They lived in a sunny two-bedroom, single-floor unit; one of five, back from the street. Although Dad worked at night he hardly slept during the day, so once I was back and we had settled into a routine, he switched to a day shift. My parents' love for each other was very evident: he bought her flowers, read her poetry, brushed her hair. Often I found them lying together on the bed, wrapped in each other's arms. After I gave Mum her morphine injection she would fall asleep, Dad sheltering her, his tears silently making a pathway to the pillow.

Aunty and Uncle lived on the other side of Christchurch and I often drove over in the evenings, swapping the sadness at home for the incredible sadness of Mum's only sister. My cousins Ken and David and Uncle Ivan helped me through those months, steadying my course, surrounding me with love. After all I had been through since I was sixteen, I was not prepared for the guilt I felt when I realised Mum and Dad had shared my pain, and had worried about me constantly.

'Nearly all of your letters you finished with "Don't worry about me",' Aunty told me. 'Your mum would ring me straight away when a letter arrived and read it to me, always relieved to hear from you. We followed your life on a map; it was all so strange to us. You were so different from Jill, and Ken and David. Your mum blamed herself; you must talk to her, Ruthie.'

And so we talked; every day we talked. We laughed, and we cried and I finally understood what my mother's deep love really meant. Mum told me about her childhood, growing up in Lyttelton with the hills behind them. Her father, my grandfather, had been a fisherman; she recalled the nights her mother would sit at the window, twisting a tiny lace handkerchief into knots with worry while the candle burnt away, waiting for the telltale lights of the fishing boats to appear around the heads. I was told the love story of when she first met my father, about the early years of their marriage, and when Jill and I came along. It was obvious that right from the beginning I was always in some sort of trouble. Maybe that's why Dad and I got on so well: we had similar personalities.

I watched her body waste away while her mind remained alert and clear in between bouts of pain and injections of morphine. Her gentle smile, which came easily when I held her hand as I read to her, is forever etched into my mind. Memories can easily be embellished over the years — details change, albeit unintentionally. Some facts are added, others forgotten, and the rewritten story becomes the truth. But as I recall the time spent with my mother, standing as a witness to her slow death, I clearly remember her bravery and inner strength; how she wiped away my tears with a gentle hand, held her hand against the side of my face with love in her eyes. My mother, more than anyone, knew why I lived such a high-risk life. She gave me the freedom to run.

When the curtains of Mum and Dad's bedroom and the lounge were opened, the morning sun settled warmly across the rooms. Dad would always say, 'Another nice day for you, love! The sun has his hat on again.' He would check to make sure Mum was comfortable, then kiss her gently. 'I'm off, Ruthie, see you tonight,' and with that he would leave for work, tucking his lunchbox under his arm, closing the door quietly. He had started to whistle again, but we all knew it was only to cushion the blow of his daily departure for Mum.

———

I WAS STILL planning to marry Matt, but no date had been set. Mum helped me make my wedding dress, in a pale yellow material covered with tiny flowers. She sat up in the bed and hand-stitched lace around the neckline with tiny, exquisite stitches. It was long, with a fitted waist, and was the most wonderful dress I had ever owned.

Just two properties along from us, in a small, cold corner formed by three adjoining fences, stood a holly tree, the only one on the entire block. It had been planted many years earlier when the area was full of trees, green and vibrant. Steadily the old weatherboard homes had been pulled down, their massive back yards bulldozed to clear the trees, shrubs and well-established gardens for new developments. Submissive owners were paid off and bought themselves a pensioner flat, where many of them lived out a lonely old age.

The holly tree was one of the few that survived the bulldozers, living to witness the 'new way of life' that was ushered in through endless rows of drab flats or units, blocks and bricks, concrete and stone, cold and colourless. Then fences were built, tall and bare, guarding what little privacy each owner was allowed. The lower limbs of the holly tree had been removed so the fences could tuck tightly around the trunk, leaving little room for regrowth.

Mum would pull herself up in bed each morning so she could look across to the holly tree, the quiet bystander. 'Good morning, Holly Tree,' she would say. 'Both of us have survived another night.' She loved watching the sun change the colour of the leaves, the birds coming and going; it became a beacon for her.

Late afternoon, Mum would hear Dad's whistle and I could see the joy in her face, the flush of colour in her cheeks. I would sit her up on the couch with her hair brushed, and face and hand cream smoothed into her thin skin.

'How's my love today?' Dad would ask her as he came in the door, knowing full well that every minute a little more life was being taken away, not only from her, but also from him.

Then one evening he said, 'I just heard from the neighbour that they're going to chop the holly tree down. Seems a real shame — it's not harming anyone.'

Mum was stunned, tears filling her eyes. 'Surely not!' Mum and the tree had lived in harmony over the past few months; the thought that it too was going to die was too much for her.

'Ruthie, go and see them, find out what's happening,' she pleaded.

I went to the house, one of the last original wooden homes, and knocked on the door. I was greeted by an elderly woman wearing an apron, glasses low on her nose. 'What can I do for you, love?'

'It's about the holly tree. I heard they are going to cut it down.'

'Very sad, isn't it? But apparently the new owners can fit another flat in if it's removed. I've sold the property — I can't look after the house or garden any more.'

There was a sense of resignation about her.

'Is there any way we can save the tree?' I asked.

'No. They told me it's too old to move and apparently it's cheaper anyway to chop it down. But they won't do it until after I am gone — I got them to promise at least that.'

I told her about Mum, and how important the tree was to her. Then I left before the elderly woman could see my tears.

Dad shook his head when I told him. 'Don't tell your mum yet.'

Dad wanted to be alone with Mum for the last few weeks of her life so I booked my flights to Papua New Guinea. Matt was delighted; he had been waiting patiently for ten months. We had set a date for our wedding, which would take place a few days after I arrived in Rabaul.

I taught Dad how to give Mum her morphine injections;

I fussed over how to arrange her pillows, how to massage her hands and feet, and showed him how to record everything for the doctor. He took leave from work for the duration.

The day I left, I felt empty, exhausted, crushed. Mum had told me this was what they wanted: time together to say their goodbyes, and she was happy that, at last, I was to settle down with a man as special as Matt. 'How many men would have waited so long, Ruthie?' she asked. 'He loves you; now go and love him back.'

Uncle and Aunty drove me to the airport, leaving my father on the doorstep looking hunched, haggard and beaten down. We hugged and he thanked me, and then in his usual abrupt way he said clearly, 'On your way!' With a half-smile and sad eyes, he turned and closed the door.

CHAPTER 15

SLIPPING AWAY

Leaving New Zealand again, this time with my mother dying, felt like closing yet another door, shutting out the light, totally blanking out my emotions. In many ways I welcomed the darkness, which allowed me to cast aside painful memories and move on.

My antidote to such sadness was more adventure and more risk-taking. I feared nothing; the worst that could happen was that I would die.

I was aware that constant chaos was now my norm. My only way forward was to block out my past, focus on the future and keep moving.

Matt was waiting for me at Rabaul Airport. His smile

was so openly honest and full of love. I fell into his arms and wept tears of happiness, shame — and confusion. We were so different. Three years younger than me, he had waited for me for almost a year, never questioning our relationship. Everything was organised for our wedding on 1 June 1972, in three days' time. On that day, surrounded by friends, I became his wife.

My mother died four days later, on 5 June, but I didn't find out until I received a telegram on the 7th:

Mum passed away peacefully 5am Monday lovely funeral today Love Dad Jill Colin and Aunty

Some memories are so clearly etched in your mind that when you recall them, there are no spiderwebs, no misty clouds. I recall sitting on the side of our bed with Matt, holding the telegram, then closing my eyes, remembering Mum's face, hearing her voice, feeling her touch, even sensing her smell.

Although we had said our goodbyes, the telegram filled me with despair. I knew Mum would not have died peacefully. I had witnessed her suffering, especially just before I left.

Death was such a frequent visitor in my life. I had learnt to block out the tearing pain before it consumed me and plunged me into depression.

The Department of Aviation supplied Matt and me with

a house, and with it came a Haus Boy called Peter, a Tolai, who are the indigenous people of the Gazelle Peninsula. The word 'boi' was used by British colonists for indigenous men, and was adopted by the expats. It was banned in the 1950s and was replaced with the English spelling, 'boy'. I was against having a servant but it was expected: we were giving work, wages and accommodation to a local. Peter lived in a concrete hut with a dirt floor in our back yard. He cooked outside and washed in a bucket around the back of the hut. It seemed wrong, with us living in a two-bedroom home filled with every comfort and convenience.

Many locals chewed betel nut, the sweet seed of the areca palm, which acts as a stimulant. It was known as 'buai', and was chewed together with a mustard stick dipped in slaked lime powder (calcium oxide mixed with water). The betel nut stained their mouths red, rotted their teeth and caused oral cancer. It's still a popular local practice; according to the World Health Organization, nearly one in every 500 new cases of mouth and oropharynx cancer worldwide is in Papua New Guinea.

Rabaul has never really been a Tolai town — it was very much an expat town, built to witness colonial power. Papua New Guineans and the Chinese lived on the outskirts, with their own shops and shanty buildings. Having made many friends among the Chinese community during my first stay, I was quickly welcomed back. Some hoped I would resume my role as 'the penciller' and join the card evenings, but I was now a married woman and had Matt's reputation to consider. It felt a bit risky to return to working for an illegal bookie.

It was just after our wedding that air traffic controller Rod Thomas and his wife Pam came to Rabaul. Pam and I formed a fast friendship that is still strong today. Although we were very different, Pam was a huge support to me, with my 'stroppy, out there, "take no prisoners" attitude', as she described it. She was very glamorous, with long blonde hair, an amazing figure and a fantastic wardrobe (she worked in a small fashion shop in Rabaul). Pam was always there for me but, despite our closeness, I never told her my backstory. There was too much to unravel and I only ever wanted to look forward and go, go, go.

I worked initially at the Cosmopolitan Hotel, but then I was offered work as assistant nurse and driver to orthopaedic surgeon Dr Marion Radcliffe-Taylor ('Mattie'), a New Zealand woman who had lived in Rabaul for over twenty years. She had graduated from medical school in 1922, 'in the days when female doctors were considered doubtful characters', she once told me. She worked in Dunedin Hospital as a house surgeon and then travelled to London, hoping to qualify for admission to the Fellowship of the Royal College of Surgeons. When she discovered that women were not allowed to attend the lectures in London, she went to Edinburgh. She briefly returned to New Zealand with her qualification, then headed for

Western Australia. After a failed marriage she travelled to Papua New Guinea in 1954. As an ardent feminist she was incensed that women did not receive equal pay for equal work so set up her own private practice in Rabaul, specialising in orthopaedics.

Mattie and I became great companions, both willing to push the limits, neither of us accepting the 'norm'; that was when I recognised that I was a feminist. Women everywhere were standing up demanding equal pay, challenging male-dominated careers and — yes — throwing away their bras. 'Why on earth are you wearing a bra, Ruthie?' Mattie asked me a few weeks after I started working for her. 'Get rid of it!' And I did, except when I was wearing light, see-through clothing or playing sport. I was thankful I had a small bust.

We travelled by car all over the island of New Britain holding clinics in the villages, delivering babies, setting broken bones. Mattie carried out small operations and handed out medication. The World Health Organization had contracted her to collect water samples, as they were investigating the spread of the two mosquitos, one of which carried dengue fever and the other malaria, both quite common. We took quinine sulphate tablets to prevent malaria but there was no preventative medication for dengue fever. A large part of our work was educating the local villagers on how to protect themselves and keep their water clean.

I became known as the 'liklik meri dokta' (small lady

doctor) while Mattie was the 'gutpela tumas dokta' (best good doctor). Even though everyone knew Mattie, I was under strict instructions that if I ever had the misfortune of running anyone over I was not to stop, because the payback system could see us killed in return. We always travelled with the car doors locked.

After the 1972 PNG general election Michael Somare formed a coalition government that promised to lead the country to self-government and eventually independence. Many expats in Rabaul decided to leave, fearing that the writing was on the wall for the 'colonial dictators'. However, apart from some small uprisings, life basically went on as before for us; we were never threatened. Mattie was delighted that she was witnessing the independence of the people she had grown to love over the years.

Mattie held surgery five days a week. She was an extra-ordinary woman: full of energy, driven to helping people and often working for no payment. It was interesting, some-times exciting work — until Mattie fell ill with encephalitis and was urgently flown back to Australia. She never returned, which would have been devastating for her.

I have never forgotten Mattie; many decisions I made in my later life were seeded at the time when I worked with her.

After Mattie left Rabaul, I decided to open a small café beside the Travelodge. My first expense was the lawyer's fee:

To my professional costs of acting for you on the purchase of coffee shop in Travelmal Building, including preparation of Deed of Assignment, attending on execution by all parties application for business name and reporting to you thereon.

It came to NZ$38.54. Stamp duty was $1.

The very official Deed of Assignment, a huge three-page document stamped with the Common Seal of Rabaul Motel Pty Ltd, was signed on 8 July 1974.

The Appletiser was open for business! In the first 12 weeks my sales were over $7000 — net profit $1080. The average annual wage in Australia in the mid-1970s was around $7000 so I was extremely happy. I only opened for six hours a day and did all my own baking, and the café quickly became very busy, often full to capacity.

With Cat Stevens, Diana Ross, The Beatles and Elvis Presley playing in the background, I produced food from a tiny kitchen that was big enough for only two people. Lunchtimes were crazy, frequently chaotic. I was training two local girls as assistants. Pam, my dearest supporter and friend, recalls a day when I told her to shut the door mid-rush and tell everyone I was closed. It may well have been one of the days when we ran out of food, as one of the girls had forgotten to buy supplies from the market.

During this time I received positive news from my father. Dad had a couple of lady friends after Mum died;

Left My parents, Howard and Freda, on their wedding day in 1944.

Below The Hobday girls: me (left) with Mum and my sister, Jill.

Above My 1954 class photo at St Mary's School in Christchurch. That's me with the wide smile on the end of the row (far right). I'm about eight years old.

Below Fun and games at Pile Bay in the summer holidays: me (left) and Jill (right) with our cousins Ken and David.

Left A studio portrait in my navy uniform, mid-1960s.

Below Me (left) with Jill and Mum, celebrating Jill's twenty-first birthday in 1965.

Above On board the sloop *Islander*
in the South China Sea, 1971.

Below The four armed pirates who boarded
the *Islander* as we sailed towards Jakarta.

Left Me with my faithful dog Jericho (Jerry) and a wallaby I was rearing in Armidale, New South Wales, late 1970s.

Below Boris the boar soaking up the sun with me and Michael, my business partner in the Armidale piggery.

Above Life at sea on *Magic*, the 30-foot yawl I purchased in 1981.

Left Me and Jerry sailing *Magic* on the east coast of Australia.

Left Skippering a tourist vessel for Fiordland Travel (now Real Journeys) on Lake Manapōuri in the mid-1980s.

Right A cherished photo of my son Andrew as a baby. We were reunited in the late 1980s, when he was in his twenties.

Left Me and Lance on our wedding day, 7 October 201? We were married by the Southland District mayor Frana Cardno.

Below Two Wee Bookshops and The Snug (far left).

he was a true romantic and courted them with dedication and determination. He was inclined to tell wee white lies about his age, so when I first met Brenda, the first girlfriend, she was obviously surprised to learn that I was only a few years younger than she was . . . From then on she called my father her 'knight in rusting armour'! Brenda was a marathon runner and had a beautiful German shepherd. While she was running, Dad would wait at the finish line with the dog, fulfilling his promise to be her loyal support crew as long as he didn't have to run anywhere.

After Brenda, Dad met Joan through her brother Gibby, a friend from Naseby days. Dad went into full courting mode to ensnare Joan, with bunches of flowers, boxes of chocolates dropped off in her letterbox, and well-choreographed Sunday drives. Joan had been a widow for a few years and Gibby thought Dad might be the answer to getting her life back on track, as well as Dad's. And it worked!

I was in Rabaul when we received the wedding invitation, which came as a huge surprise — I hadn't realised he was in a serous relationship. Matt and I flew to Christchurch for the wedding. Matt would be meeting my family for the first time, on his first trip to New Zealand. Dad was glowing — full of laughter and jokes and even doing little dances around the house. It was the happiest I had seen him for ages. Joan was a very serious woman and a dedicated Catholic, so they married in the church. She was a terrible cook but Dad helped out and they became a great team.

My own love story with Matt was going well; our relationship was strong and we lived in a supportive community. I played squash, joined the South Pacific Lager hockey team, started the Rabaul Rangers — a branch of Girl Guides for teenagers — and I wrote children's stories for the local newspaper, the *Island Trader*. We had a wonderful social life and went on holidays to the Solomon Islands and Australia, including Tasmania.

I had everything that any young woman could want, including — and especially — an incredibly understanding husband.

My life was full, with not a minute wasted. The café had grown to the extent that I had employed another expat to help me with the baking and overall running of the business. But in amongst all the happy action I could feel myself slipping. I couldn't understand why suddenly I couldn't sleep. I was starting to drink heavily — Bacardi and Coke, Golden Dream cocktails and cheap wine. Was it because Matt's contract was about to finish and we were starting to plan a life in Australia? Or because we were talking about starting a family? For the first time I started to feel fear.

Over a very short time my life changed completely. The house of cards I had built on top of my past was collapsing — again. Instead of working it through with

Matt and talking to my friends, I sold the coffee shop, packed up four wooden tea chests and walked out, leaving Rabaul overnight.

I was back on the run.

TALES FROM
THE BOOKSHOPS:
PLEASE REFER TO THE SIGN

———

ON THE CORNER of Home Street and Hillside Road in Manapōuri I have a sign reading 'Open'. It's also written on a blackboard sign outside the bookshops.

On this particular morning I was sitting at the small desk in the main bookshop. The shelves inside the bookshops were full, the shelves outside were full and the doors to both bookshops were wide open.

A middle-aged American woman came to the door, stood on the doorstep and leaned in. Before I could say anything she asked, 'Are you open?'

I hesitated for a few seconds as she looked at me *inside* the bookshop, through the *open* door. I smiled and said, 'Yes.'

'Oh!' She looked surprised. I was surprised that she was surprised. And then a follow-up question: 'Do you sell books?'

How does a bookseller, surrounded by books, reply to this question? My brain jumbled and I wanted to say, 'No, this is a butcher's shop.' But I just looked at her and eventually she turned and walked away.

CHAPTER 16

DO NOT
GO GENTLE

I checked into a hotel in Brisbane, intending to stay only one night before continuing on to either Sydney or Melbourne to find work. The tea chests with my belongings were being shipped to Sydney, where I had arranged for them to be stored for an indefinite period. The single large suitcase I had with me was bursting with clothes and a few precious belongings — enough, I reckoned, to get me started again. I was 28.

But with no plans in place, and my most recent heartbreak all too fresh, my mind filled with memories of Joshua, and the imposing cemetery where his tiny body was laid to rest. I felt the crushing pain that went along with those memories. Here I was, back in Brisbane. How could I not go and see his grave?

I caught the bus to the cemetery, sitting by myself halfway down the bus, the only other passenger up the front, chatting happily to the driver. Heavy rain in the normally sunny city had kept people inside, even though it was a public holiday. My hands kept twisting my pale blue handkerchief into a tight knot, evidence of my rising unease.

The bus stopped, the brakes squealing on the wet road. 'This is your stop, madam,' the driver called down to me.

I climbed down the steps and hoisted my umbrella. Although I was dressed for the autumn day, I still shivered as the mid-morning rain painted a depressing picture of the outer-city suburb. The rain splashed around my high leather boots, and the bottom of my long raincoat darkened as it became wet.

I had done my best to remain calm and controlled on the bus, but as soon I was off it I was overwhelmed by emotion. I started sobbing, gasping loudly with each breath. I threw the umbrella aside and the wind caught it and tossed it across the road. My walk turned into a slow jog; then, with a driving sense of desperation, I began to run towards the cemetery, faster and faster. But when I reached the top of the hill I felt a reluctance; my feet became heavy. With effort I raised my head, wiping aside the mixture of rain and tears. The Catholic cemetery loomed in front of me.

From the roadside, people easily formed the impression that this was a resting place for the elite. Large brick shrines stood boldly, with false pride, just back from the pathway. Locked glass doors shut out vandals but invited the curious to gaze upon the wealth of the Italian families buried here. The Giovannis — Bruno, Maria and Anna — had their resting places marked out by long cold slabs of marble.

Beyond a polite space of green grass lay the ordinary gravestones of the common folk with their quieter messages of grief, love and sorrow. The presence of stone angels, crosses and the occasional bowed figure of Our Lady still clearly showed that this was a place of Catholic burials.

Enormous though the cemetery was, I knew exactly where to find Joshua's grave. I became increasingly furious as I walked past the expensive death houses, the imposing shrines, the grand monuments and the pretty white stone pathways. The orderly rows of graves followed the slope of the hill as it sank down, out of view from the road. At the bottom of the hill was common ground, with the graves of the people who could not afford a plot. Two small rows of plain white crosses stood forlornly against the overcast sky.

By now I was completely soaked, my hair stuck in heavy strands to my face and neck. Hunched over, as though carrying an enormous load, I slowly made my way down the hill. The further I went, the softer the ground became, until near the bottom the surface was saturated. The moist earth squelched under me; my boots were covered in mud.

Finally, I reached him. I stopped, raised my head and closed my eyes. My anger washed away as the tears ceased. Opening my eyes, I gazed down at his small wooden cross, now slightly lopsided in the swampy ground. The miniature rose I had planted was struggling to survive.

I reached down to touch the cross and read the tiny brass plate.

Joshua 13½ hours old.

Brief, just as his life had been.

I threw back my head and screamed at the sky. All my energy deserted me as, like an old drunk, I sank to my knees and wept. The pain, grief and loss that I had been trying to outrun finally overwhelmed me and I wailed. I screamed out to the thousands of dead that lay around me, howling against the silence of the still morning. No one could share my pain. I felt so alone.

I don't remember how long I stayed there, crouched and crying in the rain, but eventually I started to shiver. My muddy hands were white, my fingernails tinged with blue. I felt completely disconnected from the world around me.

The sheer despair of the surroundings filled me and an uncontrollable urge took over my entire body. I wrapped my arms around the wooden cross, my Joshua's cross, my fingers clawing at the wood as I tried to yank it out of the ground. 'You'll come with me!' I shouted. 'You'll not stay in this bloody swamp!'

The thick mud finally gave up ownership and the cross was out of the ground; the roses too. No one witnessed my broken figure as I staggered back up the hill with the cross. Madness had chewed a crazy pathway into my mind.

Back at the top of the hill I turned and looked down to where I had been. Joshua's burial place lay bare, a small patch of nothingness. Only his tiny body remained, hidden in a swamp of so-called peace.

I stumbled out onto the road. I must have been a horrific sight but if anyone turned to stare I didn't notice — and I didn't care. My only thought was that at last I had something tangible to connect me to Joshua.

I tripped and fell, the cross laid across my body. With effort I lifted myself, both arms clasping the white cross. A passing car stopped and a woman stared at me wide-eyed as she wound down her car window. 'Can we help you?'

The driver quickly got out of the car and came around to where I stood. He shook his head as he took in my wet clothes and my muddy face and hands. I was shivering and crying uncontrollably.

'Come on, lass, let us help you.'

My vacant eyes, unable to focus, looked straight through him.

'What's this you've got?' he asked gently. 'Seems a strange thing for anyone to be carrying around.'

I didn't resist as he helped me into the back seat of the car, clinging to the cross as though it was a sick child. He struggled to fit it into the car, lying it half across my knees and angled up against the roof.

'Where shall we take her?' asked his wife, sounding slightly panicked.

'To hospital — or maybe the police. Try and talk to her. Maybe she'll say something.'

'I don't know why you stopped — she makes me feel uncomfortable. She looks mad. And what's with the cross?'

He drove carefully through the rain, his eyes constantly looking up to the rear-vision mirror, which he had adjusted to watch me huddled in the back seat.

'Stan, see what the plaque reads?' said the wife, as if I couldn't hear them. '"Joshua 13½ hours old". Do you think it was her son?'

'Maybe . . . ask her.'

'I don't like this. Just drop her off,' the woman whispered too loudly. 'It's none of our business. Stan! Stop the car!' She was becoming hysterical.

Reluctantly he pulled over, turned and looked at me, the sorrowful sight in the back of his car. 'I want to help you,' he said to me, speaking very slowly and clearly. 'Can you understand that? Would you like to get out here?' He looked at me with genuine concern, and then reached over the back of his seat to hold my hand. My impulse was to shrink from the physical contact, but then I clutched his hand tightly.

'I'll take you wherever you want to go, but you must tell me,' he said.

I felt the warmth and strength of his hand. My mind began to clear and I suddenly realised what I had done. A soft feeling of peace and clarity settled over me like a mist.

'Can you take me to Nudgee Road, please?' I asked.

Shocked at the sound of my voice, the woman turned back to look at me in fright. But the man smiled and nodded kindly. 'As good as done, lass.'

I looked straight at the woman; our eyes met. 'It's all right,' I whispered to her quietly. 'I'm not mad. Not now, anyway.'

When we arrived at my motel, Stan took the cross and stood beside the opened car door for me to get out.

'I'll carry this in for you — won't seem so strange,' he half-whispered to me. His wife stared at us.

We walked together to my room on the ground floor, Stan striding alongside me carrying the cross as though this was something he did every day.

'Anything else I can do for you?' he asked as he propped the cross up against the small table. 'Are you going to be okay?'

'Yes, I think so. He was my son. Joshua was my son.'

'I thought as much. What are you going to do now?'

'I need time to think.' I stepped towards him and gave him a hug. 'Thank you so much, Stan.'

He hugged me back: a big man with a big hug. 'What's your name?'

'Ruth.'

'Well, Ruth, it's been an experience I'll never forget. Take care, lass.'

I collapsed on the bed and slept for hours.

When I woke I went out and bought a huge hessian sack. I placed the wooden cross in it, tied it securely with rope, and headed out to the airport with the sack and my suitcase to catch a flight to Melbourne. From Melbourne I boarded a flight to Canberra, for the sole reason that it was the next flight out with a spare seat.

———

SLOTTING INTO A new place, building a new life, was second nature to me now. I had a system perfected by repetition. I booked into a hostel in Canberra, bought a newspaper and within a few hours I had a job interview at a hotel at Queanbeyan, out from the centre of town and just across the state border in New South Wales.

The head chef interviewed me for the position of early-morning kitchen hand and breakfast cook. I would work with the pastry chef 4–7.30 a.m., then switch to cooking breakfasts until 9.30 a.m., then help prepare salads and desserts for lunch. The shift finished at 2 p.m. I knew it would be busy enough to keep my mind occupied, which was the only way I could keep moving forward. It suited me perfectly and I got the job.

I found cheap accommodation: a small, self-contained unit built into the back of a garage. It was quiet and, more importantly, I could be by myself. Next I sorted my transport. There were no buses running so early but I'd seen a shop selling second-hand motorbikes. Why not? I thought. I'd never ridden one, but the price was right.

The owner sold me a Honda Z50J, and after an hour-long lesson he was happy for me to ride it home. I was so excited that when I started the bike the first time I turned the throttle too hard. The front wheel lifted off the ground and I raced out of the yard, totally out of control, balancing on the back wheel. I learnt that lesson quickly.

The baker I worked with, Marek, was Polish; his English was about the same level as my motorbike skills. With our limited communication we worked well alongside each other making pastry for pies, baking cakes and biscuits, and whipping up yummy cold puddings. We also made the fillings for a hundred pies a day — half of them meat, the rest apple.

Marek thought I would struggle with the huge mixers, the large saucepans and the massive trays, but I proved him wrong. On the third morning he gave me my own

45-centimetre wooden rolling pin. The overall length including the handles was 66 centimetres, and the handles were fitted with ball bearings so it weighed well over a kilogram, but I was determined to make it work.

As we got to know each other, Marek and I worked together quickly and quietly, our rhythm only broken when he happily threw flour at me. We hardly spoke, both buried in our own thoughts. I often wondered if Marek was as tormented as I was: two broken souls making pies at 4 a.m.

'Root,' he said, using his version of my name as he mixed Belgian biscuits one morning, 'you are like spice. Some mornings like chilli, ginger, pepper or curry, other mornings like cinnamon, or cardamom.'

'And this morning? What am I this morning?' I asked.

He looked directly at me. 'Like me, you have eaten an onion,' he replied. 'No spice, just full of tears.'

He was right. Many mornings I just wanted to cry until there were no tears left. I thought about Joshua's death; my mother's death; about where my adopted son could be; and of course, Matt, the husband I had walked out on. I was full of guilt and struggled to find anything I liked about myself. I wasn't drinking or smoking or doing drugs, even though they were readily available at the hotel. I only ate out of necessity.

I had pared my life down to the basics: my bike, my job, and long visits to the library. I devoured the classics:

O. Henry, George Eliot, Oscar Wilde, Chaucer and the dark and moving poetry of Dylan Thomas:

> *Do not go gentle into that good night,*
> *Old age should burn and rave at close of day;*
> *Rage, rage against the dying of the light.*

Thomas wrote this famous poem when he was in his thirties and it was first published in 1951, only two years before he died of pneumonia. His words kept me alive through a really dark time. I was now operating on automatic, in a state of depression with thoughts of suicide constantly pricking my brain. I had lost my courage. I was full of rage.

On the morning Marek told me he was leaving and starting up his own small bakery, I threw a basin full of flour at him. He stood looking at me, his head and shoulders dusted in white, his eyes wide, like a snow owl's.

'Root! Hot pepper! You should be happy for me.'

Shaking my head, I whispered, 'You are my anchor, Marek.' He didn't understand what I was saying, but I told him anyway. 'I will leave as well.'

We had never touched each other until that morning, when he came around to my side of the huge wooden table and pulled me into his chest. We held each other, both weeping, not knowing each other's story but both sensing that we had walked similar paths.

Two weeks and a thousand pies later my motorbike was sold and I was on the bus to Melbourne together with my one suitcase, a large hessian sack tied with rope and a healthy bank account.

I had already secured work, having applied for the position of housekeeper at a Catholic presbytery in the suburb of Ashburton. I had found another place to hide.

TALES FROM
THE BOOKSHOPS:
COVE, THE BOOKSHOP DOG

——

REGAN IS A young cray fisherman who lives in Manapōuri with his dog Cove, a black half-breed with beautiful white socks, a white tip on his tail and a white chest. Cove is fourteen years old — we call him Million Dollar Dog as he is a regular visitor to the vet; in fact I think by now he half-owns the building!

When Regan goes crayfishing, we often look after Cove. He learnt very quickly that when the bookshop bell rang there would be someone waiting for me to open the shop, but more importantly, someone to pat him and tell him how beautiful he was. He often got there before me; by the time I had reached the shop he was already lying down in front of his new friend getting patted.

Everyone takes photos of Cove. One woman who was travelling alone wanted to borrow him for the day as she was convinced he had fallen in love with her. I couldn't bear to tell her he was like this with everyone. He is such a bookshop hero that he even gets his own fan mail.

When I first opened my bookshop, it was named 45 South

and Below. One day a letter arrived addressed to COVE, c/- 45 South and Below Bookshop, PO Box 40, Manapōuri.

Next a parcel arrived by courier, addressed to 'Ruth and Cove, 1 Home Street, Manapōuri', from a dog-lover customer called Ken, who had two dogs — an old black Labrador named Nina who is deaf and blind, and Arthur, a young English pointer. Ken has written a memoir about Bluff publican Murray Flynn, proprietor of Flynn's Club Hotel. Titled *Calling My Bluff*, it had only a small print run and the last two copies went to the Invercargill Library. When Ken turned up from Invercargill to buy books, he was smitten by Cove, so he sent him a dried pigskin chewing bone.

Then another letter arrived from Aleida and Grant, who live in Havelock.

'We loved visiting your shop and browsing for books. And we loved Cove! I hope he gets to welcome people to your shop (and receive pats) for many moons to come.'

We replied to all of Cove's correspondence, including sending a photo to Aleida. In response, Cove received a bag of nibbles.

Sadly, Cove now has arthritis and is also deaf, so he doesn't hear the bell ringing. But he is always right beside me when I am in the bookshops and can be found napping out on the grass on a sunny day.

CHAPTER 17

THE MADHATTER'S MANSION

S t Michael's Church in Ashburton, 12 kilometres south-east of Melbourne's business centre, was built in 1932. The presbytery, located beside the church, was where I now lived with the parish priests. Father Philip Smith was a gentle, sincere man, and Father Michael was younger, full of enthusiasm, with an amazing talent for singing.

I had become a recluse, happy to work all day and then hide away in my small flat at night. Father Smith encouraged me to go out, to join groups such as the local chess club and squash club. But any social engagement gave people the opportunity to ask me questions I didn't want or know how to answer, so I always retreated. Everything I projected about myself was purely superficial. Internally, I was in a very dark place, with busy days that led to lonely nights and sleep full of recurring nightmares.

But somewhere along the way I met a man named John and we formed a strange kind of friendship in which I called all the shots. He wanted a girlfriend; I wanted a friend. Although I recoiled from having a physical relationship, I yearned to be held, to soak up the security of knowing there was 'someone else'. On Sundays we would explore the suburbs of Melbourne, listening to music as he drove so I wouldn't have to hold up my end of the conversation. We walked in parks, wandered along beaches, explored museums and galleries. The closest we got to any form of intimacy was holding hands. John was patient, willing to be my quiet friend for as long as it took for me to be willing to allow it to progress further.

John had very aggressive eczema — his medicine cabinet was full of lotions, tablets and, I had noticed, a bottle of a liquid that helped him sleep.

It was a Sunday, my day off, and John was away for the weekend with friends. I cannot recall exactly what led to this series of events but, in John's absence, I took the bus to his house and let myself in with the spare key I knew about, went straight to the medicine cabinet and removed the bottle of sleeping liquid.

Locking the door behind me, I walked to the station and caught the first train into the city. I sat on the steps up to St Paul's Cathedral, having no plan, just watching the people walk by on the clear sunny day as I went through the few things in my pockets. I threw away a letter with my name and address on it and cleared all other means of identification out of my purse until I was left with a little cash and the bottle of sedative.

A bus pulled up near the Flinders Street station, just across from the cathedral. Without any thought I jumped on board and paid for a ticket to the last station, which happened to be Frankston, in the south. From there I boarded a smaller bus going to Rosebud, a small seaside town.

I felt I was on a merry-go-round that would not stop and was spinning further and further out of control. Near the end of the bus trip I started to drink the sedative — slowly to start with, as I needed to get to somewhere no one would find me. It tasted bitter so I bought some peppermint chewing gum from a small shop and kept drinking the liquid.

Rosebud beach had small sand dunes partially covered in grasses. The last thing I remember is lying down in the hollow of a dune, hidden away from the road, the warmth of the sand on my legs and above me the pale, water-coloured sky. The sun was just starting to set.

Some time later I jolted awake.

'Can you hear me?' Someone was shaking me but I couldn't focus. 'Can you hear me?'

The voice sounded distant but I could feel someone lifting my eyelid. A person was speaking to me, but as I couldn't form any words it was easier to drift back into unconsciousness. The voice was persistent, however. 'What's your name?' At this I opened my eyes and focused on the crowd of people surrounding me, all dressed in white. It took me a while to register that I was in a hospital, hooked up to machines.

'What is your name?' a nurse asked slowly and clearly as she held my hand.

'Ruth.'

I can't remember much else until I woke up properly and found myself in a small single bedroom, attached to a drip. A nurse smiled at me. 'Hi, Ruth. You're in Melbourne Hospital and today is Monday. Are you hungry?'

I burst into tears. All I could think was that I hadn't wanted to be found. I didn't want to be here. When another nurse came in and gave me an injection, I slipped easily back into oblivion.

There's little to recall of the next few days, but I do remember sitting high up in a building, near the window, overlooking central Melbourne. I had a sketchpad on my knee and, with a pencil, was drawing the skyline of all the multi-storey buildings. I still have that drawing, now copied over in black ink. On the back I have written: 'Drawn two weeks after attempted suicide, from Melbourne Hospital.' Where did those two weeks go?

I was in the psych ward, a four-bed ward with three other women. Across from me was Maria, an Italian lady who was receiving cranial electrotherapy at least twice a week. Beneath her placid exterior she was a seething cauldron of fury and violence. After a series of shock treatments she went home as placid as an old cat, her eyes dull and her hair oily.

Beside her was Angie, a young woman who tore up the daily newspaper every day into small strips. She was a drug addict and prostitute, mother of two children by the time she was eighteen, both of whom were now in state care.

And next to me was Peggy, a middle-aged English woman who was regularly admitted for alcoholism and drug dependency. Kind, thoughtful, outspoken, brazen and with a quick temper, Peggy made me feel welcome as soon as I arrived. 'Don't worry, pet, it's not so bad here. They put us back together so we can go out and do it all again!'

After a few days she started to call me Ghostie, as I walked around in silence. I had been given a pencil and paper so I started writing everything down — page after page of notes describing this strange new world I found myself in.

We were permitted to walk up and down the corridor but not into any of the other wards, some of which were men's wards. It was compulsory to attend group therapy, relaxation classes and an assortment of activities such as painting, jigsaws, chess, knitting or making cane baskets.

I wanted to read but there were hardly any books besides a Bible.

During group therapy we were encouraged to talk about our own situation. Many of us were there because of chronic depression and attempted suicide. I heard that a young couple going down into the dunes for a cuddle had found me unconscious and sought help. I never found out who they were or how they managed to get me to a hospital. Initially I was furious at them, but looking back now, I only wish I had had an opportunity to thank them.

Each morning the nursing sister would briskly walk the length of the narrow corridor. In her sharp, monotone voice she called into each small ward, 'Exercise time! Look alive!' This was so jarring as most of us wanted to be dead; looking alive was not in our life plan.

The door at the end of the corridor was guarded by a thickset warden dressed in white, a heavy bunch of keys hanging from his belt.

Slowly the corridor filled with an assortment of bodies. We drifted towards the activity room, where our morning exercise routine was belted out with fake enthusiasm by a staff member. The room was mainly used for group therapy. This was where the confused bashed their heads up against the walls, and the desperate tried in vain to lift the bolted-down chairs or kicked the steel legs of the tables until their toes were as damaged as their hearts and souls.

In various states of dress and undress we gathered.

Some of us were still in our pyjamas, men sometimes with flies open and gaping. Buttons were missing as patients vacantly twisted them until they broke the cotton. One woman was dressed as though she was off to see the prime minister, carrying her handbag, her face painted with gaudy earnestness.

'Ready for deep breathing this morning, everyone? The sun is shining so let's smile . . . A nice big smile. Stretch those face muscles.'

Only a few of us took the exercises seriously. Others laughed and mucked around, while some just stood with their mouths slack and open, heads to one side. Bravely the staff pumped their way through the routine, and with each change of movement they shouted, 'Well done! Great job! What fun!'

We each had regular appointments with a psychiatrist. I have kept the following letter I wrote to mine:

> Perhaps, just perhaps, it isn't the patient, but the psychiatrist who is less than normal. But what is normal? Conforming to type? If so, what type? Who sets the type? So once again I ask you, isn't it possible that the psychiatrist is actually the patient.
>
> He too has a subconscious mind, just as active and secretive as yours or mine, but he has one

distinctive advantage, he is sitting in the doctor's chair. The party is being held at his place so, as he holds the strings, no one is ever rude to the host. How many times has he thought, as the patient rambles on nonchalantly, that he too has those thoughts? He too has those fears? Maybe it should be him sitting in this chair, fighting away the tears, chipping the varnish off the desk, ripping away at paper tissues. Possibly his nightmares are as vivid, bathing in perspiration and then the long painful hours of insomnia. Those too are his.

So who is the patient? I'm all right, Doctor, but are you?

Reading this now I can see clearly that I wasn't all right, but once again, I was trying to take control. Either way, my medication was increased at that point.

John tried to visit but I didn't want to see him. Possibly I felt guilty. Father Michael, the young priest from the presbytery where I had been working, came to see me each week, and it was he who gave me a card with a handwritten quote from *The Velveteen Rabbit* by Margery Williams. The book was to become one of my favourites. I still have his card, which I have re-read many times, and it always brings me to tears.

Part of the quote reads:

It doesn't happen all at once. You become. It takes
a long time. That's why it doesn't happen often to
people who break easily, or have sharp edges, or
have to be carefully kept. Generally, by the time
you are Real, most of your hair has been loved
off, and your eyes drop out and you get loose in
the joints and very shabby. But these things don't
matter at all, because once you are Real you can't
be ugly, except to people who don't understand.

MY SILENT BEHAVIOUR was well known by now. One day Peggy told me she'd had enough. 'Today's your big day, Ghostie. You can read us all that stuff you've been writing down,' she laughed as she dragged me along with her to the group therapy room.

After finishing his notes for that morning the doctor looked up, glanced around at the group and asked, 'Has anyone else got something they would like to share?'

That was when Peggy, my kind-of friend, looked directly at me. 'Come on, lass. It helps to talk.'

I whispered, 'I shouldn't be here.'

Everyone turned to look at me. It was the most I'd said since I'd arrived.

'I shouldn't be here. I'm not mad — I knew what I was doing.' I looked around for understanding but all I saw was vacant faces, some with tears, others smiling. I saw, very clearly, the insanity of it all.

'So Ruth, you think trying to commit suicide is normal?' asked the doctor.

'Yes, under some circumstances.'

'Don't you understand you were planning your own murder?'

'Yes.'

'So murder is all right?'

'It's different,' I replied, raising my voice. 'Don't you see what you're doing? You're trying to make me think I'm insane.'

I stood up and went to leave the room but stopped when I heard someone else start speaking. His name was Adam. He was much younger than me and his life was an even bigger mess than mine: a stepfather who sexually abused him from a very young age, the death of his mother he never loved and who never loved him, and life as a male prostitute trying to survive on the streets. Adam had attempted suicide on numerous occasions but he could not convince the doctors that he wanted to go. Like all of us he was sedated, and he was also undergoing electrotherapy, which he hated.

'I agree with her,' he said. 'It isn't murder, it's something far beyond that. I know because I've been there, many times.' He looked at the doctor, his blue eyes serious. 'She is right: we're not insane but if we stay in here we will be.'

Some other patients nodded in agreement.

'I see it like this,' Peggy chimed in. 'The staff are trying their best to get us well. We get three meals a day, a clean bed at night, we can wash every day — better than during the war in England. It's a Madhatter's Mansion: we're all a little insane, even the nurses and staff.'

Questions started to fire around the room as everyone joined in.

'Who judges the level of madness?'

'If we're all mad, who can tell what is normal?'

'Is normal being insane?'

'That means to be sane you have to be insane.'

'If the staff are insane, then we must be running the group!'

'I like being mental. The dictionary says it means "done by the mind, performed without the use of written figures". That isn't mad.'

As though a little panic alarm had gone off in her head, the nursing sister clapped her hands and called for attention. 'Thank you all for this group discussion, which was *so* interesting and has raised so many questions to think about. Now Dr Johnson has something to say before you all go to lunch.'

The doctor looked up and smiled with practised perfection. Adjusting the papers on his knee, he began to read. 'Peggy, you can go home this weekend. Make an appointment to see me in a fortnight's time. The same goes for the following people . . .' and he read out a few more names, before continuing. 'A list of names has been placed on the board for those of you who have weekend leave. And this afternoon, for everyone who is able, there is an outing.'

'Where are we going?' someone asked.

'You're going to the zoo.'

This seemed fitting.

———

DURING MY TIME in the hospital I had noticed that my heartbeat was sometimes irregular — at times I would be gasping, feeling breathless and faint. The doctor said it was arrhythmia caused by my overdose and that it was nothing to worry about. He prescribed me medication to take if I felt an episode coming on, and said I would have this issue for the rest of my life.

'Just make sure you always have the tablets with you, don't get too stressed, don't smoke or drink alcohol, and eat well.' I didn't smoke — or drink, at that stage — but the previous few years had taken their toll. Clearly it was not just my mind that had been struggling to cope with the stress, but my body as well.

The hospital was a stressful environment. We were on the fifth floor and for obvious reasons all the doors were always locked. Nevertheless, every single day Adam checked them. Then one day he found the door to the balcony had been missed — either that or he'd worked out how to manipulate the lock. No matter; the result was the same. With no hesitation, Adam ran straight out onto the balcony and jumped off.

When we were told Adam had died by suicide, I was happy for him. For him, it was the only way out of the hospital without being turned into a vegetable.

Two weeks later I was discharged. I still often think of the people I met there, who, in their own ways, taught me so much about life and sanity.

TALES FROM THE BOOKSHOPS: THE LEGACY OF BOOKS AND THOSE WHO LOVE THEM

———

THE GREATEST JOY I get from the Children's Bookshop is witnessing the bond that books weave between the children and their mothers, fathers, grandmothers and grandfathers. When a child clutches a book they really, really want, they are not only given the gift of a book, but they have been set on a lifelong path of fantasies, tall tales and true stories.

In time they may read to their own children, possibly from the book they themselves were given as a child from the Wee Bookshop.

There is one grandmother, Margaret, who comes in nearly every day with one, two or three of her many grandchildren. She sits and reads to them, gently encouraging the little ones to turn the pages carefully, then quietly sitting beside them on a small chair while they choose a book to buy or borrow.

Sadly, Margaret's ten-year-old grandson Toby recently died of cancer. After she told me, I sat on the doorstep and felt devastated. Another of my regulars had also recently died; he was in his fifties, which was young enough, but this smiling little boy who loved books . . . it was too much. After some thought I decided to have a plaque made for Toby, to hang above the Children's Bookshop door. I selected an oval shape, with a photo of Toby placed on a yellow background, and the words 'One of Toby's happy places: The Children's Bookshop'. I discussed the idea with Margaret, and later received the following note from Toby's mum:

Dear Ruth

Mum told me about your conversations — thank you so much for keeping Toby's memory and love of reading alive! Toby's brothers (Felix and Oliver) made some ANZAC biscuits to share.

Love Carolyn and Ben, Felix and Oliver and Fern and Toby, always.

I chose the colour yellow for the plaque as I wanted it to project happiness, not sadness. The wording was not to read as a memorial but to reflect what Toby loved. He will now always be part of the Children's Bookshop. Every morning when I open the door I say, 'Hello, Toby,' and remember this happy ten-year-old boy who absolutely loved books.

CHAPTER 18

MARRIAGE, MARIJUANA AND THE MENAGERIE

Upon my release from the psychiatric ward I was welcomed back to St Michael's. Father Phil had employed someone to replace me as housekeeper but he offered me use of the flat for as long as I wanted. I had a pile of mail waiting for me that I had not been permitted to receive while I was in hospital, including letters from Dad and his new wife Joan, from my sister Jill, and from Steve, a friend who had been a regular at my coffee shop in Rabaul. He was now working in Madang (still in PNG) and had written to me to tell me the position of office manager at the Madang Hotel was vacant and I should apply.

I rang the hotel and was offered the position over the

phone. I organised for Joshua's cross to go into storage with my tea chests in Sydney, and as soon as my entry permit arrived I packed up my few belongings and was on my way back to Papua New Guinea.

Unlike so many of my sudden moves, this one felt as though I was going home and I was excited. PNG was a place I understood and in many ways loved. Maybe I now qualified as one of the expatriate misfits?

Steve had a small flat and I moved in with him. We both knew there was no future in our relationship but it was easy, with no expectations. A couple of months after I got there his contract finished and he was off back to Australia. I moved into the hotel's staff accommodation.

The Madang Hotel was the local watering hole, frequented by expats and the men who worked up in the outer regions of New Guinea — as builders, teachers, seamen, plantation managers — on their days off. One of them was Tony, a blond-haired, blue-eyed Australian electrician. Our relationship developed slowly, establishing a close friendship. But there was a complication at hand — I had missed two periods since Steve had left. A quick trip to the doctor revealed I was pregnant . . .

The doctor in Madang recorded my medical history and told me very clearly that the blood condition that had ended Joshua's life would also fatally affect this baby and any future pregnancies. The only option was a termination and, at the same time, a tubal ligation so I would not conceive again.

I was stunned, but there was also a sense of relief that the matter had been taken out of my hands. I had been terrified I would lose another child. I no longer considered myself to be a Catholic, and I had developed a strong feminist attitude, so I agreed to have the termination. The doctor had assured me it was my only option and wanted to carry it out as soon as possible.

Within two days I was no longer pregnant and my tubes had been tied.

Tony, who was now living and working in Madang, was there for me, no questions asked. He picked me up from hospital, looked after me, and held me when I cried.

I was 29, Tony was 26 and he was the exact opposite of Matt, my last serious relationship. There was a sense of wildness and adventure about Tony, and he was also a dope smoker. I had given up smoking of any kind when I was fourteen, after a very short experimental period that my father dealt with most successfully — making me smoke an entire packet of Matinée cigarettes one after another until I was violently sick.

My reintroduction to the cool, calm world of marijuana was Tony blowing the smoke into my mouth, slowly and seductively. Everything I had been told and read about 'dope' was now open to question. It was so long since I had felt any sense of peace but with marijuana I finally experienced a release. I slept soundly, there was no hangover, and I felt great!

When Tony's contract expired, we decided to go back to
Australia and get married. I wrote to my father and also to
Father Phil Smith in Melbourne, telling them about my
plans. I still have Father Phil's reply, dated June 1976:

> *It was good to receive your letter and to know
> that you are well and fully occupied with the
> excitement and satisfaction of someone to
> share your life with. I waited a little while
> before replying, but your letter contained a great
> deal typical of yourself and in it all a search for
> reassurance which I would certainly like to be
> able to give.*
>
> *You are not 'your ordinary person' or 'young one'
> for that matter. Your sensitivity is much greater
> than an ordinary person, so your perception
> is acute and in your case the potential for
> unselfishness is exceptional. Could it be though
> that unless you control and contain this
> potential, your sensitivity will be bruised again?*
>
> *Life is not a situation of perfection, which is
> something I have to keep reminding myself
> about, but one's own personality has to be firmly
> anchored if it is to find peace. In your case the
> need for a twin anchor is greater than most.*

How right he was. When I re-read this letter years later I saw that in fact all his concerns did go on to become reality. In deciding to follow Tony back to Australia I had once again cast an anchor that soon started to drag.

I had been thinking a lot about Matt, who I had left without any explanation. Through Pam, my dear friend from Rabaul, I knew that he had been devastated. I sincerely hoped he would find happiness and marry someone who loved him in a way he truly deserved. And yet when the divorce came through I felt empty, extremely sad, totally lost.

What better to fill the void than a new relationship? There would be no looking back — it was on to the next episode, the next drama.

I was embarking on a new life married to Tony.

———

WE STAYED WITH Tony's parents in Sydney until we found a small block of land with a quaint two-bedroom cottage, a large shed and two cows, up in the New England Tablelands near Armidale. Our property was at the end of a dirt road, surrounded by gum trees, with one large paddock leading down to a small stream. We relied on rainwater, which was collected from the roof into a large tank. Our only toilet was outside, quite a distance from the house.

I loved the area, the house, the cows (one of which I milked), and we quickly added a dog and two cats to our family (back then I didn't realise that cats had such a devastating effect on wildlife). I wasn't scared of the huge huntsman spiders, with a leg span of up to 12 centimetres; the poisonous red-backed spiders that liked to live in the outhouse; or the occasional snake, which, we realised, were more scared of us than we were of them.

Tony was working as an electrician and I found work at an engineering firm, keeping their accounts, doing wages and general office work. After a while on the job, learning about the steel framework construction of commercial buildings, I moved into a full-time position working on the construction drawings. It was exciting, interesting work and was the start of what was, initially at least, a happy time in my life after so long on the run.

Tony and I were married in his parents' back yard in 1976 — just a small wedding for family, including the baby kangaroo I was rearing, who wore a red ribbon for the occasion. None of my family came. We wore classic hippie clothes, Tony in flares and a kaftan top and me in a long green and white dress and sandals, my hair studded with flowers.

His parents bought us sensible, practical wedding presents — sheets, saucepans, towels and mixing bowls. My father bought us a large white pregnant sow! I named her Howard, after my father. I often wondered how many other women were given a pregnant pig as a wedding present . . .

Howard turned out to be a very bad-tempered pig who destroyed fences, dug up the waterhole, demolished her house minutes after Tony had built it and generally demanded continuous attention. I was convinced she needed company so I searched for someone else in the area who had pigs. I finally found someone who had three sows, a boar named Boris and, more importantly, room for Howard the Horrible.

Michael, from Belgium, had been in the Foreign Legion for many years before coming to Australia with his wife to live. He loved pigs. He was incredibly fit, and incredibly precise about everything. Once a decision was made, his focus was unwavering, his work ethic unquestionable. Together we decided to establish a free-range pig farm, with the four sows and Boris. Boris was a huge, gentle, black and white boar who absolutely loved everyone and everything. He didn't have a care in his small world as he was living a life made in heaven.

Eventually we formed a partnership and registered the piggery under the name Waipapa. Registration meant we were able to borrow $3000 from the bank and we bought more sows, much to Boris's delight. By 1978 we had 22 sows, 3 boars, 37 weaners and 49 suckers.

The death rate of the piglets was high due to the sows rolling over and crushing them, so I decided to design a steel-framed farrowing shed to house 12 sows. My design was simple: individual inside nesting areas opened out onto a concreted area so the sows could enjoy the sunshine. The most important addition was the farrowing rails — steel bars approximately 20 centimetres high running around the inside of each nesting area and standing out from the walls. This allowed the sow to lie down while leaving a safe area for the piglets behind her. The overall cost was just over $6000 and it significantly reduced the number of piglet deaths.

I worked at the piggery on weekends and at the engineering firm during the week. I also had part-time work keeping the accounts for a local builder. Accepting that there would be no children, Tony had thought we would spend a lot of time together once we got married. What he hadn't accounted for was the menagerie: two cats, two dogs, a cow and calf, the odd kangaroo or wallaby being nursed, and around 150 pigs!

We were very happy for the first eighteen months. Tony was busy growing a small crop of marijuana and was smoking regularly; I occasionally shared a joint. Many of our friends were smokers and we often baked a dope cake or cookies — I accepted it as just a part of our lives.

An interesting position came up with the city council: the state government was funding 'community development officers' throughout the rural communities of New South Wales. I remember going to my interview;

I had just helped load a bad-tempered sow with piglets onto the truck. I had planned to go home to shower and change but as I was running very late, my only option was to go to the interview dressed in my dirty farm clothes and gumboots and smelling like pig manure. I parked the truck outside the council office, left my gumboots at the main door and walked in a few minutes early.

Amazingly, the interview went really well; the CEO even came out to the truck to have a look at the sow and piglets. I think it might have been his interest in pigs that swung the vote in my favour: I was now the Upper Tablelands Community Development Project Officer. Here I was, employed by the local council, and my husband was growing a crop of marijuana!

I became very involved with many of the smaller communities in the area, and when I identified a problem or community concern, I set up the infrastructure to have it resolved. My work involved everything from supporting coalminers to establishing public telephone booths in isolated areas to setting up youth groups and mental health groups. The range of work was vast and I loved it.

During this time I also started studying at the University of New England in Armidale, researching drug addiction, alcoholism and women's health. If I was to live with drugs, I needed to know how to survive that.

—

TONY'S MOTHER HAD warned me before we married that her son had a bad temper, but I only witnessed the occasional outburst during the first eighteen months of our marriage. He never hit me but he threw things, including the ironing board. He would become verbally abusive, cursing and shouting and then collapsing and begging forgiveness.

As his violence increased I became scared of him, but this was my third marriage and I was determined to make a good go of it. None of our friends would have believed me if I told them what was happening — Tony was well liked, and on the surface we had a good marriage.

But after four years things had got really bad. I knew I had to leave him for my own safety, and in 1980 I did. His mother fully supported me as she had suspected for a long time that our marriage was not a happy one.

In a strange coincidence — the sort that happened many times during the writing of this book — a few months prior to writing this chapter I received an email from Tony. I hadn't heard from him for over 38 years but one of his friends had found me on the internet. I briefly replied and forgot about it. But when I started writing about our marriage I became hesitant: how much did his sister, who now had grown children, know about what happened? Did they know why we separated? I knew he had been in jail since, on drug offences, as I had kept in touch with his parents. I'd also heard he had been to counselling.

I decided to email him and ask for his telephone number, explaining that I was writing a book on my life. A reply came straight back: he was happy to speak to me.

I was nervous; I really didn't know what to expect. I wanted to write about surviving an abusive relationship but at what cost to Tony and his sister's family?

I dived in and rang the number, and to my relief we chatted easily; this was the Tony I first knew in Madang. After some time I asked, 'So what shall I write? It was all so awful — I was scared of you.'

'Write the truth,' Tony replied, much to my astonishment.

'But what about your sister, and your nieces and nephew? What will they think if they read it?'

'I was selfish. I wanted you to myself. Dad loved you and told me you were too good for me. I am so sorry for everything.'

While we were married, he had told me so many times that he was sorry that it came to mean nothing to me. Just meaningless words. Now, all these years later, I believed him for the first time. I started to cry and I could hear the tears in Tony's voice as well.

'Why were you such an angry person?' I asked him. 'Are you happy now?'

'I am content. I broke up with my partner after a number of years; I'm living by myself now with my dog. I don't lose my temper much any more. I don't blame you for leaving.'

We talked for over half an hour; we even laughed together. I now understood so much more and I felt I could put aside my anger and mistrust. Tony had wanted just me, nothing else, no one else. He had plans for our future but I was too busy to listen. I wanted more. My life was full of animals, people, work, good causes, and Tony got what little was left. The less time I spent with him, the angrier he got; and the angrier he got, the less time I spent at home with him. The cycle embedded itself into our lives until there was nowhere for us to go.

'I was privileged to have you in my life, Ruth,' he said.

Nothing will change what happened back then. But what has changed is that Tony is now content, and I have forgiven him. He is now a friend and we have so much to talk about.

The *decree nisi* dissolving our marriage became absolute on 15 December 1984. I would have loved to know, back then, that such an honest conversation would eventually be possible, 38 years later.

TALES FROM THE BOOKSHOPS: THE NEXT GENERATION OF READERS

———

MANY LITTLE GIRLS love fairytales — and tales about fairies; they see a book with a fairy on the cover and they immediately hug it. Fairytales, *which generally don't feature fairies,* can be traced back to the seventeenth century when Charles Perrault's *Contes de ma mère l'Oie* (*Tales of Mother Goose*) was first published.

Perrault was born in France in 1628 but did not start writing stories for children until he was 67. His stories included 'Cinderella', 'Puss in Boots', 'The Sleeping Beauty', 'Little (Tom) Thumb'.

One young girl, a passionate reader, came in to my shop one day looking for something different. She chose two spy books, *Spy 101: Codes and ciphers* by Kris Hirschmann and *Spycraft: The secret history of the CIA's spytechs* by Robert Wallace.

I wonder how many readers of Roald Dahl (author of *Charlie and the Chocolate Factory*, *The BFG*, *Matilda* and many other books) know that he lived a double life — one as an author and the other as a British spy? He served as a fighter pilot and an officer in the British Royal Air Force until 1940, when he crashed in Libya's Western Desert and was badly injured. After six months in hospital he was no longer able to fly so at the age of 25, in April 1942, Dahl was posted to the British Embassy in Washington DC as an assistant air attaché. While there he worked in a division of MI6 alongside Ian Fleming, the creator of James Bond.

While *James and the Giant Peach*, published in 1961, was Dahl's first novel aimed at children, *The Gremlins* (1943) claims to be his first piece of writing for children. Inspired by pilots' tales that he picked up during his time in the RAF, the story is about creatures responsible for mechanical failures on aeroplanes.

> *And above all, watch with glittering eyes the whole*
> *world around you, because the greatest secrets*
> *are always hidden in the most unlikely of places.*
> *Those who don't believe in magic will never find it.*

Roald Dahl penned these words in *The Minpins*, the final of 34 children's books he wrote between 1943 and his death in 1990.

I am often surprised at what books children read. Holly is into natural history and, obviously, spies. A number of girls around twelve years of age are reading the Brontë sisters, and one of my regular thirteen-year-olds has just finished *Tess of the d'Urbervilles* by Thomas Hardy. In 45 South and Below I hardly ever sold a classic book; now I have trouble keeping the shelf fully stocked, which is wonderful.

CHAPTER 19

A KIND
OF MAGIC

It was 1980 when I left my job at the council, and we sold our farmlet and my half-share in the pig farm. I packed up my belongings and moved to Sydney. This time I was joined by one of our dogs, Jericho, a beautiful golden mongrel, who had stood (and sat) close to my side over the previous few years. I had just enough money to buy a small yacht of my own but first my belongings, once again, had to be added to my storage shed in Sydney.

My grandmother on my father's side had been Australian. Her maiden name was Cable; they must have been a well-to-do family as they had a building and a lane in Sydney named after them. One of Gran's cousins, known to us as Aunty Jacki, had married William Greville Cross, a policeman who represented the New South Wales Police Rowing Club as bowman in the coxed eights at the 1936 Berlin Olympics. They didn't win a medal but he came home with a sapling oak tree, a gift Hitler had given all contestants.

There is an amazing book about the coxed eight teams at the 1936 Olympics: *The Boys in the Boat* by Daniel James Brown. The story is based on the American rowing team, who all came from lower-middle-class families and struggled to pay their way through school during the depths of the Depression. I enjoyed learning about the building of the skiffs from cedar, and the importance of synchronisation between the eight rowers and the coxswain. The other part of the book is about Hitler's use of the international Olympic platform to cover up the Nazis' attempted extermination of the Jews.

Aunty Jacki and Uncle Bill, both in their seventies, lived in a stately home they had built in Northbridge, overlooking Sailors Bay. Uncle Bill was a tall and strong, stern man, always immaculately dressed, every outfit elegantly finished off with a silk cravat. When they first met he was a dashing young policeman. Aunty Jacki had been a model in her youth, and became the first travelling saleswoman for an oil company in New South Wales. She drove a company car, smoked long cigarettes and dressed in the smartest fashions. Some of her wages were paid in shares so when she left the position she cashed them in and opened an antiques shop in central Sydney.

Jacki was a very beautiful, independent woman, until she fell in love with Bill, who totally dominated her for the rest of her life. Unable to have children of their own, they adopted a son, whom Aunty loved dearly. But Bill, a harsh father, threw him out of the home at an early age and forbade Jacki ever to see him again. Aunty Jacki became an alcoholic.

Once I was back in Sydney I visited them often. They were an eccentric couple, living in a house full of antiques, each with their own bedroom. Uncle Bill took a shine to me — his niece who could talk about boats and had travelled a lot. When I turned up with a male companion Uncle Bill was rude to him and cold to me. Uncle Bill had a small sailing boat that he no longer sailed and hoped to sell it to me, but I looked it over and decided it was not quite what I was looking for.

'What are you looking for, Ruth?' he asked.

'Something I can sail by myself,' I said. 'Nothing too complicated.'

I found a small flush-deck yacht: a 30-foot (9-metre) yawl with a reasonable set of sails, no toilet or shower so fewer holes in the hull, and no room for a fridge, which didn't worry me as I was by then a vegetarian. The only thing I didn't like was the fin keel. The boat's name was *Magic*! I bought it.

The previous owner helped me and my friend Paul sail her north from Sydney to Coffs Harbour. Once there, I started to prepare for my trip up to Cooktown on the northern Queensland coast. I scrubbed *Magic* clean, bought stores, itemised everything, checked the charts, radio (small boats didn't carry radar or GPS back then), safety gear, ropes, anchors and rigging. I practised lifting the dinghy off the deck into the water and took her out to get familiar with the sailing rig. Jerry would sleep up for'ard on top of the sails, tucked down safely.

The next guest on board was a wee tabby kitten who had been found on the wharf; I adopted her and named her Ludmila Hoffman. One of my favourite children's books was *Ludmila and The Lonely* by Paul Gallico, about a lonely cow. And I had just seen a film starring Dustin Hoffman. The kitten became Hoffie and absolutely loved the boat. She could sleep anywhere, even tucked in behind some books in the small bookshelf. I had a high-sided square basin that I lashed to the bottom of the main mast, sat on sacking and filled with sand — that became her toilet box. I was always amazed when, even in really bad weather, Hoffie would come up to the cockpit, check out the waves and movement of the boat, and as soon as there was a slight lull she would leap from the cockpit straight into her box. I eventually put some sacking around the sides so she could cling on while she was in there.

As for Jerry, I had a long coil of old rope that I rolled into tight coils to form a small mat. She always toileted on that. To clean it I just tossed it over the side, let it drag behind for a while, then hauled it back on board.

Paul had decided to join us, even though he knew very little about boats. I was pleased to have his company, and as there were not going to be any long-haul passages I thought he would be fine. Paul came from a Greek Orthodox family and his mother had made it abundantly clear to him that only a 'nice Greek girl' would be acceptable as a wife. Even so, we were lovers for months.

On 25 May 1981 we left Coffs Harbour. I was in my element until I got very seasick; the motion sickness tablets I had packed had not worked at all. Jerry, Hoffie and even Paul were enjoying themselves as I lay below knowing that I had 24 hours of not only vomiting but also diarrhoea ahead of me. Remember I said there was no toilet on board? The plan was to use a bucket jammed between the two single bunks — quite straightforward unless you were also vomiting . . .

There are sandbars all the way up the eastern coastline, so to enter a harbour or anchorage from the sea you have to time it right, ideally entering at the end of an incoming tide, and setting your course has to fit around the tides of the East Coast Current as it flows south from the Great Barrier Reef. It's one of the strongest currents in the South Pacific, moving at up to 7 knots per hour in certain places. When you have a small yacht that is happiest cruising along at 4-5 knots, setting a course is vital. The further north we got, the more extreme the tidal range: sometimes the tides were up to 4.5 metres.

Paul, loving his luxuries, had set up a TV on board. Throughout my diary I now find numerous comments on the poor TV reception — when we were swinging on anchor the reception reacted accordingly, as did Paul's temper. He was not a happy sailor but he hung in. I think he liked the *idea* of living on a boat but he definitely struggled with the reality, especially on such a small boat. He trolled for fish each day, carefully watched by Hoffie and Jerry, who expressed as much excitement as Paul did when he landed one.

On my thirty-fifth birthday we were anchored with other boats at Grahams Creek, a mangrove-lined tidal inlet near the south-west corner of Curtis Island. It is about 9 kilometres long and flows into the southern end of The Narrows. The height of the tide at the time was 4.4 metres, producing a strong current, so it was important to time our entry right. Because of heavy fog we had to lay over for the day, fighting off huge mosquitoes. The next day we joined a group of small yachts and a couple of fishing boats as we wove our way through The Narrows to Great Keppel Island.

By now Paul had decided that sailing wasn't for him and he planned to leave. I knew I would be happier sailing without him so that was fine by me. I think the time we spent together on *Magic* convinced him that we were not a good match, so we broke up at that point. A few years later he married a nice Greek girl.

As for me, with so many other boats heading north I had made a lot of friends — sharing meals, going ashore together and helping each other out — so I knew it would be no big deal to be by myself with Hoffie and Jerry.

After having previously spent up to ten days at sea at a time, I found sailing the eastern coast of Queensland really quite a breeze, as you could drop anchor nearly every night if you wanted to. You had the option of sitting out bad weather. I had heard that there was work for a cook at a fishing lodge near Cape Tribulation, where the Bloomfield River flows into the Coral Sea north of Cairns. I made a quick phone call to the manager and was offered two months' work; I just had to make sure I was there by the last week of August.

I anchored *Magic* in the Bloomfield River on 29 August, only to find that getting to the lodge involved a half-hour row by dinghy, then a slog through mangroves full of stingrays, crabs and saltwater crocodiles. This could not be done at high tide. Apparently crocodiles particularly love dogs so Peter, my new boss and a dog lover, organised a small boat with an outboard for me to use. Eventually Jerry, Hoffie and I arrived safe and sound.

The work was easy, with seven staff for up to six wealthy guests. I cooked breakfast and made lunches for the guests to take out on the fishing launch, then I had time off before I prepared and served dinner.

Late October I started to head south, stopping off at Cairns where I slipped *Magic* as her hull needed scrubbing. The growth on her was incredible and there were a few repair and maintenance jobs to carry out.

One of the shore workers had fallen in love with Hoffie; if she wasn't on his shoulders being carried, then she was following him around. She was besotted with him, spending the day with him before returning to *Magic* for the night. Hoffie had made it clear that her sea adventures had come to an end and she wanted to go ashore. I'm sure she didn't miss us nearly as much as Jerry and I missed her.

The northerlies had arrived, so many yachts were heading south. With steady winds of 10-12 knots, I decided to sail straight through to Mackay from Cairns, with a night's stopover at Bowen, allowing three days. The weather at first was perfect, but I was heading into a storm.

Then on 15 November the coastal area around Mackay was hit by cyclonic-force winds, lightning and torrential rain. The wind and rain disrupted power and overturned boats in Mackay Harbour. As night closed in, *Magic* was battling high seas. The reefed main had been ripped off the mast, so with only the mizzen to steady her I motored south towards the harbour entrance.

I was looking out for Flat Top Island lighthouse, which marked the river entrance as well as highlighting shoals at Shoalwater Point and a reef off Hay Point. I should have been easily able to see the lighthouse on approach, but what I didn't know was that the light had been extinguished. It took some time for me to realise what had happened but I wasn't too worried as I knew I would soon have the lead lights to guide me in to safe harbour.

But there were *no* lights — no lighthouse, no shore lights from the city and no lead lights.

I checked and rechecked my chart. I had to be near the entrance. The wind and seas had dropped so I decided to trust my instincts and head towards the coast, listening for waves crashing on the shoreline and hoping to see the shape of land. For safety, I systematically ran parallel to the coast, hoping to see a break in the wave pattern that would point to the entrance. It took nearly two hours. Just before 0200 I entered Mackay Harbour, exhausted. My entire body had been tense and terrified for hours, but I had made it.

In the morning the harbourmaster came over to see me. 'Where the bloody hell did you come from?'

We had a good chat about the events of the night. Meanwhile, Jerry leapt off the boat and swam ashore, desperate to get to solid ground. She squatted and peed for what seemed like three minutes. I sat on the deck of *Magic* and cried.

On 1 December, I sailed into Coffs Harbour. In the six months at sea I had logged up over 2800 nautical miles. It was time to go ashore again.

TALES FROM
THE BOOKSHOPS:
FINDING THE LIGHTHOUSE

—

DYLAN AND HIS mum Catherine arrived at the bookshop just to have a look around, attracted by my wee building. Dylan was eleven years old and was home-schooled. Being at home meant he was able to explore his interests in more depth. With long hair and a polite, quiet manner, he began to relax as we started to chat about his favourite books.

He had been introduced to poetry and liked the old English way of speaking and writing. Children's poems bored him, so the first poem he ever read with his mum was 'The Raven' by Edgar Allan Poe. While studying English history he read *Ivanhoe* by Sir Walter Scott, who was now one of his favourite writers.

Unlike most eleven-year-old boys, he also began collecting English bone china. After we had known each other for over a year, Lance and I were invited over to his home one afternoon for high tea. We drank tea from his beautiful English cups and devoured his wonderful scones covered in jam and cream, followed by miniature chocolate and coconut sponge drops.

Dylan was so passionate about reading that I gave him one of my old poetry books, *Poems of Owen Meredith (the Earl of Lytton)*, with an introduction by M. Betham-Edwards, dated around 1927. This was the start of Dylan's collection. When his family went to Wellington soon after he found a rare copy of Scott's *Poetical Works* — leather bound, published around 1869 — in a hospice shop.

The second time Dylan came over he was accompanied by his parents and his sister Olivia. Dylan was decked out in a dress suit with a bowler hat, his long hair tied back, and this time he had a ready smile for me. His interest in books prompted me to suggest that he come over to learn a little bit about the book trade. This led somehow to a discussion of sailing books and the art of navigation. Dylan was no ordinary eleven-year-old.

Lance was the obvious teacher. The friendship between Dylan and Lance grew quickly as they worked their way through some of Lance's old navigation charts. Dylan soaked up the new knowledge, quickly learning how to read a chart and plot courses, which required an understanding of the use of dividers, a parallel ruler, the compass rose and sundry chart abbreviations. Then they moved on to lighthouses.

I have always been interested in lighthouses. When you are approaching land after days at sea, it's always a relief to see one, confidently flashing a steady beam of light through the darkness. Even as you are sailing along a coastline at night it's reassuring to confirm your position when you sight a lighthouse. Each one has a signature light, which allows you to identify a particular lighthouse.

A number of my readers are interested in lighthouses: how they were built, the stories of their keepers and their overall history. A delightful English man came into the bookshop one day with an open smile and full of chatter, introducing himself as John. He asked if I had any books on New Zealand lighthouses. I had in stock *Always the Sound of the Sea: The daily lives of New Zealand's lighthouse keepers* by Helen Beaglehole, *New Zealand Lighthouses* by Geoffrey B. Churchman and *The Sea is My Neighbour: A lighthouse keeper's story* by T.A. Clark, which is the book John bought.

John was a member of the Association of Lighthouse Keepers, based in the UK, which is dedicated to keeping lighthouse heritage alive. He gave me his card and I have shared the details with a number of customers who have been seduced by the light of the lighthouse.

A must-read is *The Lighthouse Stevensons* by Bella Bathurst, an extraordinary story of the building of the Scottish lighthouses by the ancestors of Robert Louis Stevenson, author of the much-loved *Treasure Island* and *Kidnapped*. Between 1790 and 1940 eight members of the Stevenson family planned, designed and constructed the 97 manned lighthouses that still stand around the Scottish coast, working in conditions and situations that would overwhelm modern engineers.

Thomas Stevenson designed and built the wonderfully named Muckle Flugga lighthouse on the northern isle of Unst in the Shetlands in 1854. First lit in 1858, it stands 20 metres high and is Britain's northernmost lighthouse. Robert Louis visited the lighthouse with his father as a young man and Unst became his inspiration for the map of 'Treasure Island'.

For anyone interested in our southernmost lighthouses, there was a wonderful book published in 2010: *Lighthouses of Foveaux Strait: A history* by Angela Bain.

Go! Find a lighthouse. After learning the history of these incredible structures you too will become an avid fan.

CHAPTER 20

RESIST MUCH, OBEY LITTLE . . .

*M*agic was safely moored at Sailors Bay, Sydney, just across from where my aunty and uncle lived. Now I needed shoreside accommodation and a well-paid job. I was out of money (again).

Jerry was being looked after by a friend near Coffs Harbour who rang me to say she was pregnant to his blue cattle dog and he wanted to keep her. I knew a Sydney flat was no place for a dog who was used to an exciting life at sea, with something interesting happening every day, so reluctantly I agreed.

My first position was as a private nurse to an elderly Italian woman I grew very fond of over the year that I was there. But exciting things were happening over in Tasmania and I wanted to be part of that. I had recently read an American novel called *The Monkey Wrench Gang*, by Edward Abbey. Monkey-wrenching was a term used to describe 'nonviolent disobedience and sabotage' as a form of protest. I still have my copy: it's a hard book to come by in New Zealand, perhaps because it's still considered so controversial, so an American friend brings me copies when he visits.

If anyone is interested in becoming a protester, then this is the book to read. As well as being filled with advice, it is hilariously funny and contains beautiful literary quotations from the likes of Richard Shelton and Thoreau. Some wise words from Walt Whitman resonated with me: 'Resist much, obey little . . .'

Their words clung to me long after I had finished the book. I decided it was time I stood up for what I truly loved: the oceans, the forests, native animals and birds. All these things seemed to represent the essence of who I was.

I think it was my mother's father who planted in me the seeds of care for our environment. We would row the boat out from Pile Bay into Lyttelton Harbour and sit fishing, sometimes in total silence and other times he would tell me stories. When we had caught enough fish for our meal he would slip the oars back into the rowlocks and we would head home.

'Leave enough for tomorrow, Ruthie,' was his fishing

motto. When we dug for pipis and cockles, or collected oysters and mussels off the rocks, we took only what we could eat straight away. Today there are no shellfish left at the bay, only a few undersized pāua around the coast.

Later on, when I was in the navy, I joined a small anti-whaling march down Queen Street, but it wasn't until the late 1970s that New Zealand moved from being strongly against whaling to being positively devout.

In 1978 the Tasmanian Hydro-Electric Commission announced plans to build a dam on the Franklin River to generate electricity. Tasmanians were divided over the proposal; many supported the project for economic reasons, while others opposed it because the proposed flooding of the Franklin River valley would irreparably damage an environmentally sensitive wilderness area.

I was following the debate in the newspapers, and observed the anti-dam movement growing throughout Australia. Bob Brown, director of the Tasmanian Wilderness Society, put his hand up to lead the movement to stop the construction of the Franklin Dam. In 1982 he toured Australia raising support, and David Bellamy, the famous English environmentalist and botanist, joined him in speaking to over 5000 people in Melbourne and then again in Sydney. After hearing them speak, I was ready and willing to take part, however I could help.

A blockade of the dam site was planned for 14 December, the day a UNESCO committee in Paris was scheduled to list the Tasmanian Wilderness Area, which included the wild rivers of the Franklin and the Gordon, as a World Heritage Site. I planned to be there.

I arrived at Hobart, together with many other interstate protesters, a couple of days earlier, and soon learnt that volunteers were wanted at the dam site near Warners Landing. There some 2500 of us gathered with the intention of trying to stop the unloading of bulldozers, and to block the entrance to the proposed work sites.

I was full of adrenalin, ready for whatever might happen: we had nothing to lose. There was a great feeling of comradeship — we knew we weren't standing alone and this was incredibly powerful. It was as if everything that had happened to me over the previous few years had made me strong — not brave, but resilient, willing to accept the consequences.

In the few days I was there over 1500 protesters were arrested (not including me). Bob Brown was amongst them; he spent nineteen days in jail. The day after his release he became a member of Tasmania's parliament.

Even David Bellamy was arrested, according to a news-sheet from one of the protest groups:

> Bellamy, with great gusto, made a special trip
> to Tasmania in 1982 to join the Tasmanian
> Wilderness Society's growing campaign to
> stop the Franklin River being dammed and its

*rainforests, caves and wildlife drowned. His
arrest at Tasmania's Franklin River blockade
made world headlines.*

We knew it had become a federal issue in March 1983, when a campaign in the national print media helped bring down the government of Malcolm Fraser. Bob Hawke, the incoming prime minister, had promised to stop the dam from being built but the fight was not over until 1 July, when a High Court ruled in favour of the federal government in *Commonwealth v Tasmania*. The protection of the Franklin River was sealed. The many thousands of people who protested had won.

In 1985 another 'monkey-wrenching' book was published, edited by Dave Foreman with a foreword by Edward Abbey. I didn't come across a copy of this book until 2019. *Ecodefense: A field guide to monkeywrenching* covers everything from tree and road spiking to billboarding, fence-cutting, making smoke bombs and stink bombs, and jamming locks. The book was initially banned in Australia.

Here's a snippet from the introduction to the second edition:

*4) Read, study, memorize and faithfully observe
the section on Security in this book. It will keep
you out of jail unless your luck is just plain bad.*

5) Finally — go out and do something. Pay your rent for the privilege of living on this beautiful, blue green, living Earth. Monkeywrenching will succeed as a strategic defense of the wild only if it is enthusiastically and joyously undertaken by many individuals in many places.

I was now a dedicated greenie, monkey-wrencher and activist. But first I had to replenish my bank account.

TALES FROM
THE BOOKSHOPS:
WELCOME, KATHERINE MANSFIELD

———

THREE YEARS AGO I found a tiny baby bird outside the bookshops, eyes closed and near death. I spent many days encouraging it to feed and keeping it warm, and soon soft down started to sprout all over its body, giving it a rather comic appearance. I didn't even know what type of bird it was until sometime later when new feathers displayed the beautiful patterns of a thrush. We called her Birdie.

Over the following month she learnt to fly and to feed herself and eventually became completely at home with us. Birdie sat on top of my computer when I was writing, then on top of my sewing machine watching with interest as I took up the hem of a pair of jeans. She clung to the curtain rail over the sink calling for food, and when she was tired she nestled into Lance's neck to sleep. If I went outside, Birdie would fly behind me, sitting on the clothesline as I hung out the washing, or working alongside me in the garden, seeking grubs; she was my constant companion.

We were outside walking around our small forest when

Birdie flew off and didn't return for a couple of days. When she reappeared she chirped loudly for food so I placed a small dish of mince on the kitchen windowsill. She devoured it quickly before flying off again. Each day Birdie would fly through the window, sit on the sill and eat her mince, then disappear. It was a wonderful outcome: I had raised this wee bird from near death to a magnificent thrush who was now free.

Then, one day, after about a week of mince on demand, she didn't return.

Three years later I opened my bookshops, set out the books on the table and school desks, put out the OPEN sign and sat down to work on my computer. A thrush approached the door, stood near the doorstep and started to demand attention with some enthusiastic chirping. I was surprised because thrushes are normally very timid, but here was this bird staring straight at me and demanding a response.

Suddenly I realised. 'Is that you, Birdie?' I asked. I ran into the house and grabbed a small amount of mince from the refrigerator. We always have thawed mince on hand, as we feed Mrs Brown, a female blackbird who has been visiting us for four years, and her husband Mr B, who sometimes calls in for 'takeaways'.

The thrush was extremely happy to have the mince and, after feeding herself, gathered up a beakful of food and flew off, over the fence and into the forest. Maybe this was Birdie, and she was taking food for her babies?

I couldn't believe she had come back after three years. Over the next few days she reported in regularly, feeding and then carrying food back to her young. If I ignored her she became extremely loud. It was Birdie, no doubt about it.

I renamed her Katherine Mansfield ('Katie' for short), and she is now the Bookshop Bird. She struts around fearlessly, chirping loudly for mince when hungry. Everyone loves her and many take her photo. Katie always poses like a professional model, gazing straight into the camera.

When I am busy in the bookshop she sometimes stands on the doorstep watching as I talk to customers. She flies into the kitchen where she spent so much time as a fledgling, follows us around the garden, and bathes in the pond where she had her first bath.

After a few weeks of this her young were obviously fledged and the mince we give Katie is now for her alone. She has time to sit in the tree outside our lounge window, joining Mrs and Mr B.

CHAPTER 21

FIGHTING FOR THE OPPOSITION

The Sydney City Mission was advertising for a youth/ welfare officer at its youth crisis centre in Kings Cross, aptly named 'The Opposition'. I found brilliant accommodation, house-sitting a two-storey home that overlooked Lavender Bay, for a television advertising producer who was always away filming on different locations. I had the full run of the house and, in return for low rent, I did the housework. I bought myself a car, retrieved my belongings from storage, including Joshua's wooden cross still wrapped in the hessian sack, and started work at 'the Cross'.

Kings Cross has long been a location associated with the

seedier side of life and my first few weeks of training were as much about getting acquainted with the area as with the regulars who dropped in off the street. Kings Cross was initially named Queens Cross to celebrate Queen Victoria's diamond jubilee in 1897. This led to some confusion with Queen's Square (located in King Street!), so in 1905 Queens Cross became Kings Cross, after King Edward II. Darlinghurst Road, William Street and Victoria Street became my stomping ground. When I wasn't at The Opposition, I was out getting to know the ugly guts of the area.

I didn't take long to gain the confidence of many of the girls and guys working the streets. I quickly learnt that the police were not to be trusted, especially the drug squad. I made some business cards and gave them out to everyone I met. Just the basics: my name, my number and the instruction to 'Ring if you need me'. I was surprised at how effective they were, so I kept making them and handing them out for many months. Often when I turned up at work someone would be waiting for me, or the phone would ring and I'd be told, 'Ruth, another call for you.'

Wendy, a 22-year-old prostitute, became my go-between. She had worked the street for years and knew everything there was to know about what was happening, who was doing what, and who to keep clear of. Wendy had standards. She was one of the few who didn't take drugs; her sole aim was to earn enough money to buy her own home and 'fuck the rest of them'.

I was chatting to her on the street one day when a police car pulled up beside us. Before I could say anything Wendy called out, 'Piss off!'

'What's up, Wendy?' the policeman asked as he rolled his window down. 'Got a new friend?'

I walked over to the car and gave him my handmade card. 'I'm Ruth, new at The Opposition, and you are?'

'Shit, another bloody religious nutter,' he sneered. 'You won't last long.'

'Try some manners — at least be decent if that isn't too hard to do,' I replied.

He leapt out of the car, opened the back door, grabbed my arm and pushed me onto the back seat.

Yes, I was scared. Wendy had warned me the police were corrupt and I knew the kind of treatment they dished out. It was only my second week in the job and I was already becoming known to the police.

'Just shut up and listen,' the cop said to me once I was in the car. 'You don't call the shots. Don't start making trouble, just do your fucking stupid job and don't interfere.'

'What am I not to interfere with, Officer?' I asked as innocently as possible.

'Christ! Just stay off the streets. Sit in your shithole of an office and write notes! Anything, but don't listen to the street trash.'

'The way I see it, I am sitting with the trash right now,'

I replied calmly, then suddenly thought, where the hell did that come from?!

The cop spun around to look at me. I stared straight at him, not breaking eye contact — what did I have to lose?

'We'll be bloody watching you. Put a foot out of line and you'll be gone. Now get the fuck out of here.'

'Thank you for the warning, *Officer*,' I said as I got out of the car. 'Have a nice night.'

Wendy had scarpered but she found me and hugged me. 'Bastards!' she said. 'Are you all right?'

'Yes, I feel more than all right actually!'

This was the start of my increasingly dangerous association with the Kings Cross police and drug squad.

———

THE SYDNEY CITY Mission offered a small number of beds, hot showers, evening meals and counselling, but our most important role was providing friendship and understanding to those who came through our doors. Many of the street workers just wanted a quiet place to rest, and a hug. I have always been great at hugging so this came easily to me. It also gave me a chance to quickly check on their weight (nearly always too thin), and smell the alcohol, drugs and often the aftermath of sex. With this information I could help them just a little more.

Simon, a young male prostitute, had found his mother

dead in her car when he was only fourteen; she had gassed herself in their garage. The smell of car exhaust made him want to vomit, he said, but he couldn't get away from it. Now nineteen, he was one of the boys who traded his body, leaning against the high brick wall waiting to be picked up by a cruising car. He sucked men off for $20, let them fuck him for $40. He despised himself; he was already an alcoholic, drinking cheap port by the flagon.

I first met Simon on Foster Lane, a nearby backstreet cul-de-sac that was narrow and unlit. Tall commercial buildings loomed above it, surrounding it completely except for the entrance. Halfway down the lane on the right-hand side I found a commercial rubbish bin with a heavy hinged lid. Street rubbish made up only a small percentage of the contents; the rest was papers and boxes, disposable coffee cups, computer readouts and other office waste.

I learnt early on that this rubbish container was an excellent sleeping place for the homeless, used on a 'first in, mine for the night' basis. This particular night it was Simon's. He had greasy blond hair, sallow skin and incredibly sad eyes.

Simon became a regular at the Mission, grabbing something to eat, having a shower, chatting for a while and then slipping back onto the street. This was just before Aids rampaged through the area, but many of the boys had already tested positive for sexually transmitted diseases and hepatitis B. Simon had both. Only months after I had found him in the rubbish container, he was beaten up so badly that he died, alone, in that very same lane.

Kathy had short black hair and a pixie face. She was tiny, with dull eyes artificially brightened up by gaudy makeup. She had run away from Perth as her stepfather was sexually abusing her. After hitching her way across the Nullarbor, she arrived on the streets of Kings Cross. Wendy brought her to me.

'She was standing on Sue's spot!' Wendy said. 'Lucky I saw her before Sue came back — she would've half-killed her.' Many of the girls had designated areas on the streets, ones they had worked hard for. There was a ranking: when you were new, you started where business wasn't so good and worked your way up.

Kathy was wearing a tight pair of jean shorts, a thin blue blouse tied up under her small breasts and high-heeled shoes. Her legs were bare. She looked so young. Wendy was appalled. 'She must be about bloody fourteen, by the look of her. Do something, Ruth!' she demanded. 'Look at her bloody arms — she's already using!'

'I'm eighteen, I just look young!' Kathy shouted, obviously lying.

Within weeks Kathy was well on the road to self-destruction. The heroin she was using cost $75 for a small amount and was often laced with rat poison. Her youth and newness to the streets meant she was immediately popular with clients, and she soon had a few regulars. At the start she made them use condoms, but they paid her more if she let them go without.

I managed to get her into a women's refuge but within the month she was back on the street. This became her cycle and none of us could get through to her, but she continued to come up to see us, often falling asleep in a chair through sheer exhaustion.

And then there was Slime. He came up the stairs to my office, and stood at the open doorway. 'You Ruth?'

'Yes. Come in, sit down if you want.' He was of stocky build, smartly dressed, clean dark hair, fingernails bitten, badly shaved. 'And you are?'

'Call me Slime.'

'No other name?'

'None that would interest you.'

'Okay.'

'You helped out one of my mates. Just wanted to check you out and thank you.'

'Have I checked out to your liking?'

He nodded. 'I've got your card,' he mumbled, pulling it out of his pocket. 'Just thought I'd ask if you can come to court with me on Wednesday. No biggie — I'm up for dealing again.'

Slime ran a group of dealers. He wasn't into prostitution — 'None of that shit for me. I help them survive that crap.'

In his mind he was doing them a favour. I learnt a lot about the Kings Cross drug trade from Slime. He told me who were the pimps, who were the main dealers and about the corruption within the authorities. Some of the dealers, Slime told me, paid the cops for protection.

For his court case, Slime wanted me to act as a character referee. 'Just say you know me and all that stuff. The police want me out on the street, not in the lock-up.'

I sat silent for a few minutes. This felt like dangerous territory. By going along with this I would basically be supporting the corrupt police operation.

'I can't do it, Slime.'

He looked down at his feet, then shrugged. 'Shit happens. Worth a try.'

The next week I was down helping serve the evening meals. Over in a far corner a group of guys were watching someone doing press-ups: '. . . twenty-eight, twenty-nine, thirty!' I went over to watch. Slime came forward and kicked the guy who was now lying on the floor. 'Think those are press-ups? Think again, shithead.'

Slime dropped down to the floor and started to do press-ups on just one arm. 'This is how you do press-ups. None of that two-bloody-arm stuff!'

When he reached 30 he looked up at me. 'Hey! Ruth! Didn't need you after all. Police dropped the charges.' He smiled, winked at me and left.

———

SALLIE-ANNE HUCKSTEPP HAD been on the streets for over ten years when I first met her. She was a good-looking woman in her late twenties. Sallie-Anne had married Bryan Huckstepp, a heroin addict, when she was seventeen. To support his habit she worked as a prostitute, first in Kalgoorlie and then in Sydney, where she too became addicted to heroin. The marriage was doomed to fail. In 1981 she met Warren Lanfranchi, a drug dealer and standover man for Arthur 'Neddy' Smith, a notorious local who had served time for drug trafficking, theft, armed robbery, rape and involvement in a number of murders.

Neddy was one of the dealers who had police protection. Many of his crimes had been sanctioned by Detective Sergeant Roger Rogerson (who, at the time of writing, is still in jail for murder). Six months after Sallie-Anne moved in with Warren he was shot and killed by Rogerson, supposedly in self-defence. But Sallie-Anne believed it was a setup and demanded an investigation. She went public with her cause and appeared on *60 Minutes* and *A Current Affair*, alleging that a team of corrupt detectives, led by Rogerson, was running Sydney's drug trade and disposing of criminals who got in the way.

In mid-1984 Sallie-Anne gave me an envelope containing information on how illicit drugs were being brought into Australia, along with the names of the people involved, including a knight of the realm, well-known lawyers, top cops and media personnel. Sallie-Anne knew her own life was now in danger. If she did happen to be murdered, she wanted me to make the information public. I promised her I would do my very best.

The heat was increasing on Rogerson and members of the vice and drug squads. Sallie-Anne gave detailed statements to the New South Wales Police Internal Affairs Branch alleging corruption, evidence tampering, bribery and murder. Eventually it would all come before the Royal Commission into the New South Wales Police Service (known as the Wood Royal Commission), but that did not happen until 1995, sadly too late to help Sallie-Anne.

TALES FROM THE BOOKSHOPS: FRANK THE TRAMPER WHO LOVES TRAINS

———

A VERY FIT, tanned German man wearing shorts, a woollen pullover and well-worn, top-of-the-range tramping boots came into the bookshop carrying an enormous backpack. His name was Frank.

He wanted a book to take on his next tramp, the Hump Ridge, and asked if I had anything on trains. I had only one book at the time but told him I had two more arriving within the week. It turned out that Frank was an author, a book dealer and a historian with his own publishing company in the small town of Berga. Frank loved trains: his business card had a train on it, his website featured a train, and he said he sold a lot of books on trains as well.

We decided that when he came off the Hump Ridge he would come and stay with us for a few days and work in our forest. We had a lot to talk about, and by then the other two train books would have arrived.

Like me, Frank called his publishing company a 'wee undertaking'. His father established the twofold business (freelance journalism and publishing books) in 2001, as he was sick of being an employee. His passion was rail transport and industrial heritage. Slowly, he came to focus on lignite/brown coal and slate mining, including industrial railways in Germany.

Frank and his father had worked together in the business since Frank finished university in 2003. He officially took over in 2014.

After years of trying he finally gained access to the photo archives of the former regional newspaper *Volkswacht* (*People's Watch*), first published in 1911. The paper had been owned by the Communist Party until 1990. The photos and the story of their survival were incredible, so they wrote a book about them!

For Frank's father, this was a journey back in time because he had reported for *Volkswacht* for ten years from 1977, writing about local history and economics. When he tried to quit in 1987, no longer comfortable with the paper's political line, he was told, 'No one quits the [Communist] Party!' Eventually he did, however, and started working for a publishing house.

Frank's father recently gained access to the historical files of the East German Secret Service ('Stasi'), and in 2019 the two of them produced a small publication about the Stasi informants working within the Party's newspaper, informing on their colleagues to ensure the content of the paper reflected communist beliefs.

Frank is now writing the fourth volume of their slate mining book series. He tracked down one of the old miners who had collected historical documents and files over the many years he had worked in the mines. He had packed all the information in spare explosives boxes. Imagine what his neighbours thought when 60 dynamite boxes were carried into his workshop!

Frank stayed with us for five days, worked hard and devoured many books. When he left, I gave him two to take with him — *A Walking Guide to New Zealand's Long Trail: Te Araroa* by Geoff Chapple, and *The Map That Changed the World: William Smith and the birth of modern geology* by Simon Winchester. I hoped the *Walking Guide* would entice him back to see the trees he planted in the small area we now call Frank's Patch.

HOME BECKONS

In September 1984 my sister Jill rang me from New Zealand. She was about to have a major operation in Invercargill and asked if it would be possible for me to come home and help look after her when she was discharged.

I arranged for a fortnight's holiday from The Opposition and flew home to Christchurch, staying with my father and stepmum for a few nights before heading down to Cromwell.

On my second day back I received a phone call.

'Hi. Don't think you'll recognise my voice but I had to ring.'

He was right: his voice rang no bells. 'Who is this?'

'Just one question before I go any further — are you still a Catholic?'

I immediately knew it was Lance. It had been seventeen years since we last spoke, on Stewart Island. 'Lance!'

I could not believe it — I wanted to laugh and cry.

'How did you know I was here?' I asked.

It was such a New Zealand story. Josie, the woman in the bed beside Jill in Invercargill Hospital, was a friend of his. The two women had got to talking and Jill mentioned that her sister was coming over from Sydney to look after her. Josie must have mentioned her friend Lance, and Jill must have told the story of my doomed engagement to a chap called Lance on Stewart Island . . . and the penny dropped. Jill gave Josie her phone number to give to Lance, and when he rang she gave him my father's phone number.

'How about I come up and pick you up? I can be there in eight hours.'

And there he was, on the doorstep eight hours later, incredibly handsome, with dark hair and a beard and the same gentle eyes. He was the man about whom I remembered every detail. And it was as though we were picking up from when we left each other on Stewart Island, almost two decades previously. Lance was now skippering a Department of Conservation vessel, the *Renown*, on the Fiordland coast.

It was an extraordinary time for both of us. I couldn't

believe he had found me. Lance had just been through a very emotional separation. Just a year earlier he had been at sea and came home to find a note from his wife saying she had left him and returned to her family in Melbourne, along with their young son, Dane. He tried everything to get his family back but failed, and a period of serious depression ensued. Then I came back into his life.

I still had the wedding ring we had had made when I was 21. Lance told me he had worn his wedding ring until it was ripped off his finger by a mooring line when he was berthing a small coastal trader up in Bougainville.

The next day we drove to Cromwell, which gave us six hours in the car to talk. After lunch at Ōmarama we clung to each other on the side of the street. I felt like I had found home, after searching for so long.

Lance had to go back to sea the next day, and I stayed for a week with Jill. Then Lance picked me up to take me down to Manapōuri. Two amazing days later I had decided to sell *Magic*, resign from my job in Kings Cross and come to Manapōuri to be with Lance. It sounded straightforward but I should have known it would be anything but.

———

I ARRIVED BACK in Sydney and began to put my affairs in order. Then I heard that a young police officer called Michael Drury had been shot twice through his kitchen window while he was feeding his three-year-old daughter. He survived, and claimed that the infamous Roger Rogerson was responsible, as Drury had refused to accept bribes offered in exchange for evidence tampering in a drug trial.

It all kicked off and gossip on the street was rife. I knew that the information Sallie-Anne had entrusted me with was enough to put away not only Rogerson but also a number of other well-known — and well-respected — people. I spoke to my Uncle Bill, who had spent his whole career in the police force, and asked if he knew of one honest cop, or anyone else, I could give a copy of the information to if anything happened to Sallie-Anne. After reading the statements he told me not to trust anyone, and instructed me to send a copy to Lance back in New Zealand, and hide the original.

But this was not what I did. Stupidly, I decided to trust a reporter I had come across often on the streets, in court and occasionally at police stations. He was writing what appeared to be very factual reports on police corruption and I felt like he would be a good ally. Together with Tim, a work colleague, I arranged to meet this reporter and told him about some of the evidence I had. It appears that that night he went straight round and told the drug squad.

In the early hours of one morning, after a busy night at The Opposition, Tim and I were walking back to our cars. As we approached we noticed that Tim's car doors were open and the car was sitting on an angle. It had been burnt out, the tyres were slashed on one side, windows smashed.

We both knew immediately we had to get out of Sydney: this was obviously a warning. My car had been left untouched so, without even stopping to pack clothes, we got in and drove through to Melbourne — roughly a nine-hour drive. Tim's sister rang work for us and said we had gone north to see Tim's mum, who was very sick. In fact we were heading in the opposite direction. We lay low for a week, during which time Lance became very concerned as he hadn't heard from me but we were too scared to make any calls in case we put ourselves, or our loved ones, at risk. Then I drove back to Sydney alone, while Tim returned by train.

On my return I rang Lance and briefly told him what had happened. He immediately offered to come over and help.

'You can't do anything,' I told him. A vision came to mind of Lance on a white horse racing down Darlinghurst Road . . . He had been a deer hunter in Fiordland so was practised at using guns, but this was entirely different. He didn't know the local forest. 'I'll come home as quickly as I can,' I assured him.

Within weeks *Magic* was on the market, my wooden tea chests and Joshua's cross were packed up and on their way to Christchurch and my car was sold. I said my goodbyes to all the friends I had made on the streets, half-wishing I could stay but knowing it was impossible. And I was being given a chance to come home and start over. After years of changing my life on a dime, I knew that some kind of stability was possible around the next corner.

But it was hard to leave the community I had made for myself in Kings Cross. Slime actually gave me a hug, and Wendy gave me a small gold ring that I still wear on the little finger of my left hand.

By December 1984 I was out of there, heading to the mountains of Fiordland, and Lance.

———

IN FEBRUARY 1986 Uncle Bill rang me to tell me that Sallie-Anne had been murdered.

Her body had been found in a pond in Sydney's Centennial Park, strangled and drowned.

Peter Smith, a federal policeman with whom she had been having an affair, testified at the inquest that Sallie-Anne was convinced that Neddy Smith and Roger Rogerson may try to kill her. The coroner found that there was insufficient evidence to place charges and found that Sallie-Anne had been murdered by a person or persons unknown. No one was ever charged.

About four years later my uncle put me in touch with a newly elected politician whom he knew and trusted. After speaking to him on the phone, I posted him the information Sallie-Anne had given me. I later declined to be called as a prosecution witness at a court hearing as I now had Lance and Dane's safety to consider. I firmly believed that Dane, living in Melbourne with his mother, might not be safe from retribution.

Although Rogerson was dismissed from the police force in April 1996, his criminal career continued: he was sentenced to multiple jail terms for various crimes. He is now serving a life sentence, alongside fellow former police officer Glen McNamara, for the murder of 20-year-old drug dealer Jamie Gao in May 2014. They lost their appeal in July 2021.

The television series *Blue Murder*, set in Sydney in the 1980s and screened in 1995, tells the story of the dealings between Rogerson and Neddy Smith. The sequel, *Blue Murder: Killer Cop*, a two-part miniseries, which premiered in August 2017, continues the story of former Detective Roger 'the Dodger' Rogerson.

TALES FROM THE BOOKSHOPS: JACK AND THE SEASONAL CONFUSION

———

'**CLOSED FOR WINTER.** Ring me if you want me to open' reads the sign outside the bookshops during our off-season. Manapōuri basically shuts down over winter. We have no ski-fields to bring in skiers or snowboarders, and many of the walking tracks are closed, so I close the shops late April and reopen mid to late September. It's a good opportunity to restock, spring-clean, and attend to any upkeep needed by the rare and old books.

Early one September I was weeding the garden outside the Children's Bookshop when I noticed a young boy, maybe ten years old, standing by the door of the main bookshop.

'It's not winter any more. Why aren't you open?'

'I'll open in a few weeks but I can open now if you would like me to.'

'So, you should have said you are closed in winter AND early spring,' he said in a serious tone.

As I opened the main bookshop, I asked him what he liked to

read. 'The Children's Bookshop is empty because all the books are stored over winter,' I said, 'but you can look around this one. My name is Ruth. What's your name?'

'Jack. I'm here with my mum for a week. You should have been open four days ago.' He wasn't going to let it go. Jack's blue knitted hat came down to the top of his glasses; he was well dressed for the cool weather.

'What do you like to read, Jack?' I asked in another attempt to divert him from my obvious ignorance of the seasons. He stood in the middle of the shop and looked around, 'Sea squirts. They are on the wharf at home. Do you know what a sea squirt is?'

As luck would have it, I did know a little about ascidians (sea squirts), as Lance was a diver and underwater photographer, and I had also dived in Fiordland, where they are plentiful.

'Ascidians. Yes, I have seen them when I was diving.'

'Wow, that's so cool!' Jack looked at me with renewed interest. I was not as stupid as he had thought.

'I have a book on ascidians in my own library,' I said. 'Let me go and get it.' Relief! I had redeemed myself.

Jack looked through the book with interest. 'Do you know that the white sea squirt is only found in Fiordland?' he said.

'No. I wonder why?' I replied.

His mother arrived; she had been down to our local shop. 'Jack has been waiting for four days to meet you,' she said.

'Why didn't you ring me? I would have opened for him.'

'He wanted to tell you in person that it wasn't winter. He

was waiting to see when you would realise it was now spring.'
Clearly, Jack's mother was very familiar with her son's manner.

'Yes, so he told me.'

I offered to give Jack the book but his mother said he could borrow it when they came back for another holiday.

As they left, I heard Jack tell his mother, 'I told her it was spring!'

Time to change the blackboard.

CHAPTER 23

ARRIVING HOME

I flew into Wellington, filled with very mixed emotions. Lance was waiting for me together with ten-year-old Dane, who had been adopted as a baby. Dane came over from Melbourne to spend school holidays with his dad: this was my new family. Lance and I hugged, laughed and cried; emotionally we were both a mess, recognising that this was a big deal. It was a whole new start for both of us. Lance was 42 and I was 38.

With my two suitcases loaded into the boot, we headed off to board the Interislander ferry to Picton to start our first 'family holiday'. It was a stressful time for me: I desperately wanted to be with Lance after so long apart, but part of me was still in Kings Cross, supporting Sallie-Anne and the other street workers.

I still didn't feel safe, constantly thinking that the chaos I had left behind would catch up with me. Was it really this easy to get away and start again? And, just as intimidating a prospect: was I *really* ready for another serious relationship?

Dane was a very handsome young boy with an amazing smile, and his constant chatter helped settle me. My own son would now be twenty years old — almost the age he needed to be to consent to me contacting him, but here beside me now was another little boy, holding my hand, confident that all would be fine. I remember telling myself this was my opportunity to change my life's course, to stop running. The image I kept thinking of was a car windscreen scattered with heavy raindrops. As the wipers cleared away the tears, I started to see, clearly, a safe pathway ahead of me.

We stayed with my father and his new wife in Christchurch, giving me the opportunity to see all my aunties, uncles and cousins. I had been away for nineteen years. 'Yes, I'm home to stay,' I kept repeating.

My father was delighted but still abrasive in his usual way. 'Just settle down, for God's sake. Don't do anything stupid. Don't upset the apple cart!'

We arrived in Manapōuri just in time to see Lance's brother Hunter get married — it was the perfect opportunity for his wider family to meet me. I felt like an imposter in many ways — only Lance's mother and brother knew anything about me — but thankfully everyone accepted me with very few questions asked. Lance's father, Lucky, a huge man with a booming voice, put his arm around me and immediately called me Shorty, a nickname that only he used, up until he died.

Over the next few weeks Lance, Dane and I carefully knitted our small family together. I would stand back in disbelief, realising that I was part of something so special, something I had searched and yearned for for so long. However, there had always been a 'but' in my life, and it was back again: deep down, I believed I didn't deserve Lance and Dane. In self-preservation mode, fearing the inevitable, I started to shut down. I yearned to be an integral part of this family but I began pushing Lance away, emotionally and physically.

———

MANAPŌURI IS A small town tucked next to a beautiful lake, surrounded on three sides by spectacular mountains and Fiordland National Park, part of the UNESCO South West New Zealand World Heritage Area. It's the end of the road: from Manapōuri you either turn around and drive back the way you came or you board a boat and travel across the lake.

Tourism was by now a big player in the Fiordland economy and as I needed work, Lance encouraged me to get my commercial launch master's ticket. I had more than enough sea time and experience so I applied to attend the six-week course in Dunedin. Lance was still skippering the *Renown*, which meant he was away from home for up to ten days at a time. He would come back for about five days before setting off again. I settled into this routine quickly and although I missed him it was a good arrangement in many ways, giving us both the time to adjust to each other.

Of the eighteen students on my course only two were women. The other one was from Stewart Island and looking to run her own fishing boat. She had been fishing with her father for many years so had incredible coastal water experience; between the two of us we had clocked up more sea miles than any of the guys. The lectures were pretty basic until we got to engineering, in which I was well behind everyone else. Thankfully, Lance gave me a hand whenever he came through to see me, and although I was extremely nervous ahead of the oral examination, I passed.

On my return home I found employment with Fiordland Travel (now called Real Journeys) as a skipper on their tourist vessels. I mainly worked on the Fiordlander class boats, which had gutsy twin diesel engines, making them easy to manoeuvre.

Each day I loaded up about 80 passengers who were

signed up for either the day trip into Doubtful Sound or the shorter trip to West Arm to visit the Manapōuri Power Station. During peak season I sometimes did four return trips a day, always praying for either fog so I could use the radar, or wind so I had a small challenge to overcome. I was always suspicious of anything that came too easily; I needed some friction to work with. I wore my wedding ring even though Lance and I were not married, as I wanted some kind of barrier between myself and the male passengers.

As I was so short, the guys in the workshop built me a small box to stand on behind the helm. After boarding and counting the passengers to ensure our numbers tallied with the office, we headed off from Pearl Harbour. Over the loudspeaker I would welcome the guests on board and do a basic introduction, including health and safety information, then chat away and point out the scenery along the way. Generally it was fun, but I was constantly asked the same set of inane questions:

'Did you sit the same exams as the men?'

'Have you ever experienced bad weather?'

'Can you use the radar?'

'Are you allowed to drive the boat in bad weather?'

'Can you put your cap on so we can take a photo?'

'What does your husband think about you driving boats?'

It all came to a head when a man came up onto the

bridge one day and started to make a play for me. He said I looked very sexy in my uniform and the highlight of his trip was having me as *his* skipper. How would I like to go out to dinner with him?

We were halfway down the lake and I had had enough. I pulled the throttles back into neutral, switched off the engines, switched on the microphone and turned to look directly at the rest of the passengers.

'I am being verbally harassed by this man and I will not continue this trip until he leaves the bridge.'

Everyone looked shocked and the man crept back to his seat, mortified.

I thanked everyone for their patience, restarted the engines and continued the trip back to base.

———

MY THREE TEA chests had arrived in Christchurch and we made arrangements to drive up and bring them back to Manapōuri. At last I had a permanent home for everything, including my precious book collection.

However, when we got there I was told I couldn't have Joshua's wooden cross as it was made of untreated timber. I was stunned. I was so close to having everything in one place after so long and, most of all, I wanted to find a permanent place for Joshua's cross.

We explained how precious it was, and asked if there

was any way I could have it back. Eventually it was decided that they would fumigate it and courier it down to me.

Our home in Manapōuri — which we have lived in now for 35 years — is a small, cosy, wooden house tucked among trees. As my precious belongings began to settle, I did as well. I felt secure and began to love the place as my own. Lance built shelf after shelf for all my books; it was a wonderful feeling to finally unpack them and place them in their forever home.

Finally the hessian sack arrived, carefully wrapped in cardboard, and there, lying patiently inside, was Joshua's cross.

Even though I was thrilled to finally have it with me, it triggered a deep depression and sense of loss in me that I really struggled with. After weeks of this, Lance persuaded me to go to the doctor. Dr Patrick O'Sullivan asked all the right questions and finally he leaned forward and asked, 'So what do you want to do with Joshua's cross, Ruth?'

'I want to have it somewhere safe, not hidden away in a sack.'

Lance and I had talked about possible options — laying it in the forest, taking it out to sea and dropping it in the ocean, or putting it in our back yard — but none of those prospects gave me the feeling I needed, that at last the journey was over.

'What about the cemetery?' asked Dr Patrick.

'I don't have a body, or ashes.'

'Maybe you don't need that — just somewhere to put the cross. How about I ring the council and find out if it is possible?'

Tears of relief ran down my face. It felt right. 'Yes, please. Please ask.'

Only a few days later Dr Patrick rang me. 'They have agreed to let you place Joshua's cross anywhere near the fenceline — not within the main cemetery but just beside it. What do you think?'

What did I think? I thought it was wonderful. 'We'll go up and find a place and get back to you so you can let the council know.' I thanked him profusely.

Lance and I found the perfect site on the southern side of the cemetery, overlooking the Te Anau basin with a view across to the Cathedral Peaks.

I rang Dr Patrick, explained where the site was and asked if I could plant a native tree beside Joshua's cross. A short time later Lance and I planted a small red beech tree, not much taller than me, on the site, and in front of it we placed Joshua's cross. The small brass plaque reads:

Joshua, 13 hours old, finally at rest.

Peter, the local Baptist minister, was with us for the brief ceremony. Finally I felt that Joshua's journey was over.

This was almost true.

———

I **REALLY ENJOYED** my work with Fiordland Travel. I kept my vessel spotlessly clean and the engine shone as I cleaned it each morning when I carried out the daily engine check. I was proud of my work and I wanted my passengers to really enjoy their trip on the lake so I aimed to run a slicker, happier boat than the male skippers.

At Christmas I hung Christmas decorations inside the boat and played carols as the passengers boarded. I wrapped up presents and played pass-the-parcel with the passengers on the way back to base, which was great fun. Often, after dropping off a group of passengers at West Arm, I would return to the Manapōuri base empty, an easy, straightforward cruise that allowed me to sit behind the helm and knit. Over the course of one season, I knitted Lance two jumpers!

We visited Joshua frequently, often taking a picnic with us. The tree was growing strongly and I knew this was the right place for him. But one day we got there and the cross was gone. I was dumbstruck; why would someone have done this? We looked everywhere in case someone had thrown it into the bushes.

But it was not to be found and I was distraught. Lance rang the council and learnt that their staff had removed it, thinking it had been placed illegally. It was sitting in their shed. When we collected it we found the main stake had been broken and the rest was starting to rot, so we decided to have a new cross made.

The decaying cross sat in our garden hut for a while. In many ways I was happy to be able to see it every day, running my hand over the rough wood and thinking about Joshua. Finally I found the right man to build the replacement. A young cabinetmaker up in Nelson we had worked with had a sign on his van that read: 'Jesus was a builder too.' I explained to him what I wanted and he made the most beautiful cross, which accompanied me as I drove back to Manapōuri while Lance sailed the boat back to Doubtful Sound via the West Coast.

We held another small ceremony, this time embedding the cross in concrete on the same site.

For so long Joshua's cross had felt like a symbol of my chaotic life — always moving from place to place, never finding peace. Now he had a home, and I had a home. There was just one final missing piece to the puzzle.

I needed to find my living son.

TALES FROM THE BOOKSHOPS: GENTLEMAN GEORGE, QSO

———

EVERY FEW MONTHS Pam Plumbly, antiques expert and auctioneer, held book auctions in Dunedin that I attended. At my first auction I was told 'Don't sit on that chair' by another dealer as he pointed to a wonderfully comfortable lounge chair in the front row. 'That's George's chair.'

I sat near the back on a hard chair and waited to see who George was.

An elderly gentleman arrived minutes before the auction was to begin. Everyone nodded a greeting as he made his way to his special chair; he was clearly known to everyone.

As I found out later, George Griffiths was a historian, writer, publisher, editor and journalist of some renown. He was made a Companion of the Queen's Service Order in 1990 and named Dunedin's Citizen of the Year in 1999. George's passion was for books and music so it was no surprise to find that he was the founder and owner of the famous shop Otago Heritage Books.

After the auction I introduced myself; he was delighted to hear that I had a 'specialist' bookshop in Manapōuri.

263

'Next time, come through to Dunedin the night before the auction and have dinner with me in my bookshop,' he beamed. 'I'll give you time to look around and I'll put some books aside for you.'

And that is how I found myself sitting at a perfectly laid dinner table, in the middle of a huge bookshop, sharing a meal with George.

He was a delightful man, semi-bald with patches of white hair and a short beard, eager blue eyes and a quick half-smile. We talked for hours while going through his collections, not only of books but also of music. I bought all the books he had put aside for me, plus a few more, some quite rare.

George spoke to me as though I knew as much about books as he did. He welcomed me into the fold. I was so overwhelmed with his generosity and by the ease with which he shared his knowledge that I nearly cried when he hugged me as I left.

At the next book auction I sat closer to the front, closer to 'George's chair'. I nodded hello, along with the others, as George walked towards his seat.

Years later, George and some of his musical friends chartered our yacht *Breaksea Girl*. They had been researching the early history of music in New Zealand. According to *The Journals of Captain Cook*, edited by J.C. Beaglehole, when Cook was in Dusky Sound in 1773 he 'caused the Bagpipes and fife to play and the Drum to be beat'. George believed this was the first European music to be played in New Zealand. To celebrate the occasion he and his friends decided to re-enact this part of

New Zealand's history by playing the bagpipes, fife and drum in Dusky Sound.

George went on to write the libretto for Anthony Ritchie's composition *From the Southern Marches*. He died in 2014 at the age of 81, leaving behind a solid record of achievement.

CHAPTER 24

THE ADVENTURES OF LANCE

In the 20 years since we had seen each other, Lance's life had been pretty full too. In fact we had so much to talk about when we got back together that it's going to take us the rest of our lives.

Having been part of the Manapōuri community for so long, Lance Shaw has quite a backstory. So, here it is.

Lance left school three times — it just wasn't his scene, as he puts it. First he left Southland Boys' High and started correspondence school, which he bailed from aged fifteen after his family broke up. He and his mother and brother worked for a season on a tobacco farm at Motueka and then went to Auckland. His mother thought Lance had potential so she enrolled him in Mount Roskill Grammar, but the country boy didn't fit into the city school and after only a couple of months he was bullied out of school.

In 1958, still aged fifteen, he got a job on the Auckland Harbour Bridge as tea boy, taking orders then making and handing out the tea for one pound a day. At first he was based in Northcote so he had to carry his bike over the open span of the new bridge on the connecting steel beams, then ride down the other side.

Every day he watched ships arriving and leaving from the harbour. It looked like an exciting lifestyle and the seed was sown.

He soon tired of making tea and became a labourer on a building site, wheeling concrete around for three times the money. His mother had moved in with an electrician and they thought Lance should take on an electrical apprenticeship. He tried it but decided it wasn't for him.

For a short time he spray-painted leather hides for shoe leather, then tried his hand at butchery. Eventually, despairing of ever finding his niche, he decided to go to sea.

First he needed a union book from the Seamen's Union. Payment of the fee gave him the right to 'stand on the corner' with a number of others hoping to be given work. Generally, the ship's first mate did the hiring. It was the first mate from the *Tiri*, a decrepit wooden scow, who offered Lance his first job at sea — as a deck boy.

The *Tiri* carried general freight up and down the coast north of Auckland, including shark livers in milk cans, kauri logs from Totara North in Whangaroa Harbour, and butter from the factory at Awanui. It was a lot more interesting than making tea. After eight months he became a deck boy on the *Karamu*, which ran the Tasman route across to Sydney. On the first trip, however, one of the crew tried it on with him. Lance jumped ship as soon as they tied up back in Auckland.

Burnt by this experience, he went back to Manapōuri and found work in the Tourist Hotel Corporation hotel in Te Anau, starting off as a breakfast cook and working his way up to third cook. He was now sixteen. With this experience behind him he moved to Eichardt's Private Hotel in Queenstown for a short period, and then tried his hand at the famous Chateau in Tongariro National Park. However, feeling his cooking skills were a bit basic for this grand establishment, he left.

Running out of career options, Lance became a salesman for Bond and Bond, selling whiteware. He started a course in salesmanship and business management at the polytech where his tutor, who worked for Te Awamutu Machinery, saw his potential and offered him a position with that firm, again selling whiteware. He quickly proved to be good at it so was promoted and given a company car, a very big deal back then.

This was the first job he held for over a year but he started to realise that if he became a successful businessman he would end up like his bosses, for whom he had little respect. He handed in his notice.

New Zealand was becoming involved in the Vietnam War and Lance decided to volunteer. His mother, Kath, was a pacifist and was horrified at the news. She arranged for him to go and live on a commune near Ngāruawāhia, where he learnt about the history of Vietnam and the senselessness of the war and New Zealand's involvement. After six weeks he came away with a clearer view of reality. The war was not for him.

In 1963, at the age of twenty, Lance returned to Manapōuri and went hunting with his older brother Hunter, shooting deer in the Fiordland National Park. A carcass brought in 1s 3d a pound, head and hocks off. With the average carcass weighing 80 pounds (36 kg), that was about £5 ($10) per beast — good money in 1963 when the average weekly wage was just under $50. Tails and velvet were paid for separately and used in Asian medicines. The money was good but the conditions — and competition — were dangerous. As helicopters were being used more, ground shooting became less profitable. Hunter joined a chopper crew as a shooter but the number of young men being killed working the helicopters convinced Lance that once again he had to find another career.

In 1964 he decided to go blue cod fishing off Stewart Island in a verbal partnership with a guy he had met. After three months fishing together his partner up and left the island, leaving his debts for Lance to settle. He struggled to find work now as the locals were wary of him. Out of desperation he took a job running a fishing boat, the *Mareno*, a job he wasn't really qualified for. He ran the boat mainly by himself, fishing around Ruggedy, on the north-western coast of the island. Luckily, he came into a run of crayfish and after eight months he had paid off the debts.

He left the island as the islanders still did not trust him, and also saw him as anti-social — all work and no play. He came back to Manapōuri to lick his wounds, and returned to shooting deer with his brother. Then out of the blue he received a call from Mikey Squires, a Stewart Island fisherman, offering him a crewing position on the vessel *Roslyn*. Mikey told him he had just bought the *Ecstasy*, an X-class sailing dinghy that had just won the Sanders Memorial Cup. Would Lance like to race it next time?

Lance was on his way back to Stewart Island.

He had been sailing for a number of years on various small dinghies; this was an offer he could not refuse. Unfortunately, with very light winds for the Sanders Cup trials on Stewart Island, the *Ecstasy* was beaten by a faster boat and didn't get to represent the island in the next Sanders Cup.

Mikey and Lance were crayfishing and trawling together for about a year, during which time Lance and I met.

When our engagement ended, Lance went to Australia

and, with 50 cents in the bank, got a crewing position on a cruising yacht sailing up to New Guinea. He worked as a bar manager in a rough pub in Port Moresby for three weeks, before boarding a small cargo ship named the *Katika* as first mate. He had no qualifications for the position but the ship's owner was desperate to get someone on board so the ship could sail. The harbourmaster asked him a few basic questions about seamanship, then stamped the requisite sheet of paper.

The *Katika* worked the New Guinea Coast carrying general cargo and copra. Lance was in Rabaul a few years before I was there . . . At the time he was still wearing his wedding ring, which we had had made out of Dad's gold when we got engaged. But while the *Katika* was berthing alongside a small wharf at a coconut plantation in Bougainville, his ring was ripped off his finger by a mooring line and lost over the side.

Most of the plantations where they discharged cargo had no wharf, so freight was transported to shore on a barge powered by outboard motors. They would swing the loaded barge over the side of the ship as she was steaming along at 6 knots, which was an extremely dangerous manoeuvre. If there was no return freight to be picked up, the skipper would just carry on steaming, leaving Lance and his crew to unload the barge and then catch back up to the ship. The skipper would not slow down for them — they had to hoist the barge back on board a moving ship.

Eventually it was too much for Lance. At the last dropoff for the day they had a lot of freight for three different plantations. Quite reasonably, the plantation managers wanted to check off all of their incoming freight before signing the bills of lading. By the time this was completed it was dark and the ship was long gone, steaming back north. A plantation owner offered Lance and his crew accommodation for the night but he felt obligated to get back to the boat somehow. So they headed off into the night, powering through reef-dotted seas chasing the *Katika*. The skipper met Lance as he climbed over the rail and asked him if he was all right. Lance stood nose to nose with him and sharply replied, 'No! I am not all right. This is my last trip.'

He was paid off when they berthed and flew back to Port Moresby.

After sitting his 50-tonne coastal master's licence Lance was offered the position of mate on the mother ship of a prawning fleet of 16 trawlers. He did that for a year, but as they were not catching enough to make it pay, the boats returned to Kuwait. He was out of work again.

Lance was still full of questions about the Vietnam War so he decided to go there to investigate for himself. While in Vietnam he met a couple of reporters: one in favour of New Zealand's participation, the other against. After speaking with them, Lance felt sure he had made the right decision in not joining the army.

He flew home and got work skippering tourist boats for Fiordland Travel on Lake Manapōuri. Then a telegram arrived from an American guy he had met in Port Moresby, offering him work on a big charter yacht, the *Polynesia*, based in Antigua in the Caribbean. He accepted the position and flew to Antigua, arriving pretty much broke, only to find that his American contact had disappeared and the *Polynesia* was so rusted she was not seaworthy.

He borrowed money from his mother to fly to Canada, the nearest British colony, as he couldn't work in Antigua without a visa. It was in the middle of winter when he arrived so there was no work available on the boats, but Lance signed up to work in Sudbury in a nickel mine. Despite careful medical vetting and a safety training course, he was the only one of the intake of 23 men who was not injured over a six-month period.

He started working 1500 feet (457 metres) underground in one of the deepest mines in Canada, reaching a depth of 7800 feet (2377 metres). They were tasked with getting mud out of the drainage ditches, then progressed to scaling — clearing areas of loose rock after an explosion. They were told that the harder you worked, the more quickly you moved up the ranks to the job that paid the most: placing and priming the explosives. The newbies were always partnered with a more experienced miner. Lance enjoyed the hard work; they were good men to work with and he was learning another trade. He eventually left with a much healthier bank balance.

From there he flew to England to meet his mother, who had gone there to try to trace her family. Lance did a bit of travelling around and seeing the sights. He was hitchhiking from London to Dover to get a ferry across to France when he was picked up by a Kombi van full of hippies who invited him back to their place. They introduced him to LSD, all the rage in the psychedelic 60s and early 70s, and he ended up staying for nearly a month. Then he joined his mother returning to New Zealand by ship.

On board, Lance met his first wife, who was returning home to Melbourne. Ten days later they tried to get married on board but it was not permitted (shades of my 'marriage' to Peter). He stayed on the ship after it berthed in New Zealand and they both went back to Australia, where they married. Several months later Lance brought his wife to Manapōuri and they both worked with Fiordland Travel for over four years. He then bought a crayfishing boat and worked out of Doubtful Sound for a few years, but without much success as he had little recent experience of commercial crayfishing. By now they had adopted Dane, and Lance didn't want to be at sea anyway.

So then it was deer trapping throughout the Doubtful Sound area. He used his old crayfishing boat for accommodation as well as transporting fencing materials to build the deer pens and carrying the sedated live deer back to Deep Cove, where he kept a Land Rover to cross the Wilmot Pass. Deer were then loaded onto the bow of a Fiordlander to cross Lake Manapōuri, and into another vehicle to take them to his back-yard holding pens. This was going pretty well when he received an unexpected tax bill for $15,000. He sold his boat and trapline to settle the account.

He was then offered the skipper's position on the *Renown*, run by the Department of Lands and Survey (later the Department of Conservation). This took him away from home again but he loved the work — plying the Fiordland coast, to Stewart Island and down as far as the Snares Islands. It was a steady income working with interesting people.

During this time his marriage fell apart and Lance fell into a depression for about three years, but thankfully he was able to keep working.

That was about when I re-entered the picture.

Lance continued working on the *Renown* for about another seven years before resigning because he was seen as 'too green'. During his time with the Department of Conservation he absorbed knowledge from a number of marine scientists and became concerned about over-fishing. He became involved with the campaign fighting for marine reserves in Fiordland, joining Earth Trust and Greenpeace and passionately promoting environmental education. Eventually he decided it was time to leave the Department of Conservation.

In early 1995 we decided to start our own charter business, Fiordland Ecology Holidays. Between us we had a huge amount of relevant experience. Lance was happiest when at sea and was one of the safest skippers I had come across. His depth of knowledge of Fiordland, Stewart Island and the subantarctic islands, and his love of the ocean and natural history, made him the perfect proprietor for an environmentally focused charter business. I also had a skipper's ticket, knew a bit about boats, and had successfully owned and operated small businesses.

We would offer charter holidays different to any others, with a strong emphasis on ecology. There would be *no fishing* on board, and a percentage of any profits would go towards environmental research. Our no-fishing policy was generally considered to be commercial suicide, as all the other charter boats offered fishing. But our focus was to promote conservation and environmental education.

First we needed a boat. After leasing the 82-foot (25-metre) sailing vessel *Evohe* for eighteen months we decided to buy our own motorsailer capable of carrying passengers to the subantarctic islands.

Lance found the perfect vessel when he went on board the 65-foot (20-metre) motorsailer *Reef Enterprise*, which was working out of Airlie Beach in Queensland. As soon as he sailed her into Nelson we renamed her *Breaksea Girl* after the ground-breaking conservation project we had been involved in on Breaksea Island back in 1988, when rats were successfully eradicated from the island. Since then, islands all over the world have used the same principles to eradicate introduced pests.

Breaksea Girl was loved by everyone who sailed on her.

Over the sixteen years we operated Fiordland Ecology Holidays, Lance went down to the subantarctic 29 times carrying film crews, scientists and tourists, assisting with their work and subsidising their charter costs.

———

AS I WRITE this we have been together for 38 years, and finally found the courage to marry on 7 October 2011.

A small part of my promise to Lance told him:

> *Today you become my husband. I want to know what you ache for, what your dreams are and what you long for. I want to share being alive and happy and at times sad. You were my first love and today I am becoming your wife. I therefore promise to care for you and love you.*

And Lance's said to me:

> *Ruth, Honey Bunny, although we have had some really testing times over the last 27 years our love has kept us together . . . No matter what,*

*I will always be there for you. It is my role in life
to promote you in any direction you choose and to
help you achieve your goals. I promise to always
try and protect you from others . . . and even
from yourself!*

Lance has kept his promise, even through some very
difficult times.

TALES FROM THE BOOKSHOPS: VINTAGE BOOKS FROM BOOKSELLER BRIAN

———

ONE OF THE other book dealers I met through Plumbly's Auctions when I had my first bookshop, 45 South and Below, was Brian Nicholls, who traded under the name Vintage Books of Dunedin.

He had a large book collection of his own, acquired over his many years as a teacher. After buying a house in Broad Bay in 1995 he worked at the wonderful Scribes Bookshop in Dunedin for two years, learning about the book trade, then left to set up a shop for himself. He pondered about establishing a bookshop in central Dunedin, but since he had a large garage under the house, he decided to set up business at home.

Building a massive number of shelves was the first priority; then he set about filling them. A neighbour's son who was studying computer technology at Otago Polytechnic agreed to build him a website and by 1998 he was in business.

Initially Brian had a lot of customers, but these days most of the business is conducted through the internet. His database now stands at nearly 15,000 books. In the past few years he has concentrated more on New Zealand-published material.

Obviously I went to Brian when I opened my first Wee Bookshop and needed to stock my half-empty shelves. Boxes of wonderful books soon arrived from Dunedin, all of which Brian generously let me pay for as I sold them.

If I have any questions about a book, no matter how rare, Brian will know the answer. If one of my customers wants a book I don't have, Brian probably does.

Bookshelves looking empty? Time to visit Dunedin and search Brian's basement, with its shelves reaching from floor to ceiling.

CHAPTER 25

FINDING
MY SON

The 1955 Adoption Act introduced a level of secrecy around adoptions that effectively prevented any contact between the birth mother and the child. We were not allowed to see our baby at birth, and were expected to return to our earlier lives after the birth as if nothing had happened. The argument was that we would quickly forget about the child, therefore avoiding the pain and grief of loss. It didn't work, of course, but we were silenced. Society did not approve of illegitimate children — adoption was a comfortable answer to a socially embarrassing and unacceptable situation.

It wasn't illegal for the birth mother to know who was

adopting her baby, but the process was designed to make it extremely difficult for her to find out. The adopting parents, on the other hand, were told the mother's name and age and would usually be given some information about her. Adoption application hearings were held in closed court and over time all court records became confidential. A new birth certificate was issued showing the baby's adopted name — clearly this constituted a rebirth! The birth mother was entitled to be given non-identifying information, but only if she requested it.

The Adult Adoption Information Act in 1985 marked the end of the closed adoption era, providing adopted adults and birth parents with access to adoption information.

Like so many other young mothers who had had no option but to give their child up for adoption, I was determined to find my son. That year my son would turn 21. As I had given birth in Wellington and had signed the adoption papers there, I had a strong feeling he would have been adopted into a Wellington family. I had stated that I wanted him to go into a Catholic home — I'm not sure why I felt so strongly about that, but apparently I did. So I had two pieces of information to start with: he was likely in Wellington and in a Catholic family.

Since 1976 Jigsaw and other adoption support groups have provided enormous support for anyone searching for birth parents or adopted children. They also started the political action against closed adoption. I joined them when my son was eighteen. I regularly received their small booklet filled with information on mothers, and sometimes fathers, looking for a child who had been adopted out. Small paragraphs of brief, vague clues: so-and-so is looking for a male child, born on this date, at this hospital.

I had written to the Department of Social Welfare (DSW) in Wellington requesting any information they held on my son and telling them I was going to start the process of looking for him. In reply I had received a letter that included all the non-identifying background information they had on file:

> At the time your son was placed with them, the
> husband was 34 and his wife 29 years. They had
> two daughters, aged 6 and 3 years. The adoptive
> father is described as being a handsome man, tall
> with black curly hair and an olive complexion.
> The file notes that his wife resembled you in
> appearance. Both are of Dutch ancestry and
> practising Catholics. The husband was employed
> as a company director and had shares in a
> business. Contact with the family ceased in
> May 1965.

There was nothing more they could tell me.

I was not discouraged in the slightest. Instead I thought,

'Well, I'll just turn up at their office.' And that's exactly what I did.

I took two weeks' leave from my work, flew to Wellington and went straight to the offices of DSW. The staff member who had written to me was surprised to see me and, initially, didn't deviate from what she had told me in the letter. She said there was nothing else she could do. I was practically begging and eventually she said, as she walked away from me, 'Electoral rolls are very good.'

I went straight to the Wellington Public Library and asked for the latest electoral roll, only to be told that I had to be more specific — which location did I want? I thought quickly. I knew the father was a businessman, so I decided then and there I would start in the centre of Wellington and work my way out. Knowing my son had gone to a Dutch family, I considered what the most common Dutch surnames would be. Thinking they might start with 'van', I slowly worked my way through those names in the listing, looking for the registrations of a Dutch businessman and wife with two daughters and a son.

Eventually I came across the 'Van der Berg' family, which included a businessman, his wife, a daughter and a son called Andrew. One daughter was missing — perhaps something had happened to her? I sat staring at the name, saying out loud over and over, 'Andrew Van der Berg. Andrew Van der Berg.' Could I really have found him so easily?

I drove back to DSW, ran up to the office and said to the woman, 'Is his surname Van der Berg?'

I knew immediately from the look on her face that I was right. Somehow, the combination of coincidence, guesswork, gut instinct and dogged determination had led me to my son.

The electoral roll also gave me their address but I knew I couldn't just turn up on their doorstep. It was important to me that they, and Andrew, wanted to meet me as much as I wanted to meet them. And they would need time to prepare emotionally.

There was nothing to stop me from actually seeing him, however, so I drove to the street, parked down the road from their home and waited. I remember thinking, 'He's twenty so he'll be at work and he won't be home until 5.30 p.m.'

Eventually I saw a tall, elegant, beautifully dressed woman go into the house, but no one else turned up. I waited until it was too dark to see properly. I felt an incredible sadness and disappointment but I had come too far to turn back now. I knew they were Catholic, so I drove to the closest presbytery and asked to see the parish priest.

The woman who answered the door wanted to know who I was, so I pulled out my 'entry card', telling her that I had been employed previously as cook for Cardinal McKeefry. It worked. She led me into the waiting room where, finally, I met Father Brian Sherry. He was a friendly and kind man. After some initial chit-chat and no small amount of hesitation, I asked him if he knew the Van der Berg family. With a gentle smile, Father Sherry replied, 'Why are you asking this, Ruth?'

So I explained everything to him. When I finished, Father Sherry smiled at me, took my hand and said, 'Yes, I do know them; they come to church here. I didn't know Andrew was adopted.'

It was a momentous moment. This man knew my son Andrew.

Father Sherry told me that Andrew was blond, he was a good son and dearly loved. He said Andrew's older sister, Jackie, had been killed in a car accident in 1984, which is why she wasn't recorded on the electoral roll. During that time Andrew had been a great support to his parents and was especially close to his mother.

Every detail about who Andrew had become was a gift — and yet somehow also strangely familiar. He was blond with blue eyes, just like my father. He worked as a builder, like so many of my cousins. Father Sherry said, after talking to me for a while, 'I can see Andrew in you. I cannot believe how alike you are.'

Despite our pleasant conversation, I could sense his concern as to what my sudden presence could mean for this close family. I explained that the last thing I wanted was to cause any distress to the family that had raised my son so well.

'I don't want to suddenly turn up and pretend I'm his

mother,' I told him. 'All I really want is to meet him.' And then I had an idea. I knew it was a big ask, but I asked Father Sherry if he would be prepared to talk to the family for me. I told him that if they said no, I would not try to contact them again.

Father Sherry asked me to leave it with him; he would keep in touch.

It was an exercise in patience. Months later a telegram arrived:

Please ring me. Brian Sherry.

I rang immediately and was told that Andrew and his family would like to meet me.

TALES FROM THE BOOKSHOPS: MY I.T. HERO

———

JUST AROUND THE corner from our place my godson Jeb lives with his mum. Oliver, his older brother and another godson, works in finance up in Wellington. Both boys have amazing brains.

Jeb is now eighteen and has always been extremely helpful to me. Up until he was around thirteen he used to help me in my garden for $10 an hour. If I needed help I rang him and asked him to come and help me in the forest. To my surprise, one day he answered, 'Sorry, Ruth, I'm not a labourer any more!'

Jeb had just won an iPad and was now dedicated to upskilling his growing interest in computers. He turned out to be an I.T. natural. It didn't matter what we asked him about computers, TVs or cellphones, he always had the answer. So I suggested that he become our I.T. man instead of our labourer. Now whenever we have an I.T. problem I email Jeb, and if he's at home he turns up on my doorstep within minutes.

Jeb was sixteen when I started to write this book. I would get up at around 5.30 a.m., make myself a cup of coffee and write through until 8.30 a.m. One morning when I opened my computer in the early hours a multi-coloured ball was dancing around my screen. Everything was frozen.

Such a frustration. I waited impatiently until 6.49 a.m., hoping Jeb would be awake by then.

06:49 Ruth wrote:
Sorry about this Jeb but I am unable to open any files.
Got up to write and tried everything. Can you just
email me what I can do. Thanks From Ruth

06:52 Jeb wrote:
Are the files perhaps already open?
Are you double-clicking on them?

(Great, he's up!)

06:53 Ruth wrote:
What are you doing up! Will check and get back to you.

06:57 Ruth wrote:
I have opened a file that was already opened and now
there is a wee multi coloured ball on it and I can't do
anything. Should I replug in the USB?

07:01 Jeb wrote:
Why is the USB plugged in? Are you opening a file from
the USB?

*If nothing else works, secondary click (2 fingers) on the
app that you're trying to use to open something (Word,
I assume). Click quit.*

(I can sense a little irritation . . .)

07:05 Ruth wrote:
No the USB isn't in.
I have clicked on Quit.
*Tried to reopen Word, it is bouncing up and down
and the wee multi ball is still bouncing around so
I can't do anything.*

07:07 Jeb wrote:
*Ok. Try clicking the Apple logo in the top right corner of
the screen, and then clicking restart.*

(That didn't fix the problem.)

07:11 Ruth wrote:
I'm in my pj's – can I bring the computer around?

07:11 Jeb wrote:
. . . Alright

(Definite reluctance!)

I jumped in the car and drove around to Jeb, who was waiting at the back door, also in his pyjamas. With a few clicks and a couple of deep sighs, the problem was solved.

4 April and the spinning ball is back. This time thankfully it is not so early in the morning.

> *08:01 Ruth wrote:*
> *Hi Jeb, that wee coloured ball is back! I can do everything on internet but can't access Word or Excel. Ideas please on how to get rid of it. Thanks From Ruth*

> *08:05 Jeb wrote:*
> *Click Apple logo (at top left of your screen)*
> *Click force quit . . .*
> *Click excel/word*
> *Click Force Quit*
> *If that doesn't solve the problem, click that apple logo again, and click restart to restart your computer.*

> *08:09 Ruth wrote:*
> *Done! Thank you! Amazing . . .*

> *08:11 Jeb wrote:*
> 👍

What a hero!

CHAPTER 26

MY
BLUE-EYED
BOY

L ance was the first person I wanted to tell this amazing news. As he was away at sea I had to speak to him via marine radio, so the entire Fiordland fishing and charter boat fleet also heard my great news.

Lance offered to go up to Wellington with me when the time came but I knew I needed to go alone. We talked through possible outcomes and I knew I needed to be prepared for anything.

'I don't care what he is. I don't care if he's in jail. I don't care if he's a drug addict. I just want to know my son as a person and I'm going to accept him no matter what,' I told Lance.

I knew from working in Kings Cross that many of the homeless and street workers came from broken homes or were adopted. A few didn't want to find their birth parents, and some who had experienced a reunion with either a birth mother or father had devastating stories of rejection to tell. I knew there was a risk of disappointment — even pain — but I didn't care.

On the day I was to meet my son I must have changed my outfit three times. I even wore makeup — something I hardly ever did — because the memory of seeing his mother walking into her house the year before was imprinted in my mind. She had looked so elegant, dressed beautifully and with impeccable posture. Andrew's first impression of me was really important. I felt like I was going on a blind date.

Father Sherry had asked me to come to the presbytery early so we could plan for any outcome. I was shaking with nerves as I walked in, but Father Sherry was calm and full of smiles. He told me Andrew's father was very excited to meet me; his mother was more hesitant, which I understood completely. Then he revealed that Andrew had asked his parents to help him find me some time ago. So they were delighted when Father Sherry told them about my visit. It meant a lot to Andrew to know I was searching for him too.

Father Sherry was sure it would go well but we had a Plan B just in case — I would wait in a side room while he talked to Andrew. I said I didn't want Andrew to know yet about the rape — that needed to wait until we knew each other better.

When the doorbell sounded, I was so nervous I was on the point of tears. Father Sherry left the room and returned with a tall, blond man, dressed in jeans and a blue jumper. Standing in front of me was a younger version of my father. Andrew looked at me as I looked at him, each not believing that this moment was real. We both burst out laughing, then walked towards each other and hugged. My body soaked in his; this was where we were meant to be. Even now, when we talk about our first encounter, the strongest memory we both have is of the instant shared burst of laughter. Andrew has the same laugh and the same big, wide-mouthed-frog smile as me.

That will always be one of the most incredible moments of my life. Here was this beautiful blond boy, my *son*, in a blue jumper that showed off his blue eyes that were the exact same shade as my father's. We didn't say very much for a long time; we just kept laughing and crying and hugging.

At long last, here we were. Over the years I had heard people describe this process as enabling them 'to put something to rest', or as finding a part of themselves that was missing. I didn't feel either of those things. It was just this incredible high of seeing this young man who was a part of me and who, until that moment, had been in the shadows of my life.

I clung to him. I was now a mother, but I knew I was a

mother who had to remain in the shadow of his family. That was fine. At least I was somewhere in his life. My only thought was thank God, I have found him and he is all right.

Andrew invited me to have dinner with his family and I accepted immediately. It was an elegant and formal affair — crisp napkins, the good china, a beautiful meal. His mother was initially shy and reserved, but once she realised I wasn't going to try to take her place she relaxed. I could see the close bond she had with Andrew and it filled me with joy. How lucky, I remember thinking, that this is the family he went to.

The next day Andrew came and met Aunty Joyce and Uncle Bill. Aunty Joyce smiled at Andrew through her tears, 'Oh! You look just like your grandfather. If only your grandmother could see you.' We were all overwhelmed. Thankfully, Andrew loved hugging as much as we did; we fitted together just like a jigsaw.

Years later I did tell Andrew about his father and the rape. I knew it would hurt but his inner strength shone through. Having been brought up in a Catholic family, he had a strong faith. When we discussed this book, my incredible son wrote the following to me:

> It is very evident God has had His hand on you
> and me and given us wonderful experiences, none
> more so than the succinct telling in your book of
> our first meeting.

TALES FROM
THE BOOKSHOPS:
THE TEAM OF BOOK BUYERS

THREE WEEKS UNTIL Christmas and the garden in front of
the Children's Bookshop is in full bloom, adding colour to the
already colourful tiny building. Books are priced from 50 cents
through to around $30 for some new books. The shelves are
full and I have two more boxes of books cleaned and priced,
ready to refill any spaces.

My sister Jill is my main buyer of children's books. She is a
qualified teacher and managed the Cromwell Day Care Centre
for many years. Now retired, Jill has filled her life with volunteer
work, mainly as the manager of Operation Cover Up in Central
Otago, organising knitters for the many blankets they send
overseas every year. And once a week you'll find her at the
Cromwell Hospice Shop. She spends hours knitting, felting and
making the most amazing children's garments, blankets and
wall hangings. When we travelled together around Southern
Ireland she sat beside me knitting while I did the driving — she
quite literally knitted her way around Ireland.

When I needed someone to source and buy second-hand

children's books, Jill was the obvious choice. After a bit of guidance she jumped in with such enthusiasm I had to slow her down! Box after box of books arrived at the bookshop and I had to remind her I only have room for 150 children's books, not 500! She sighed. 'I know! I just can't help myself!'

Every charity shop within 50 kilometres of Cromwell knows Jill. The recycling centres in both Wānaka and Alexandra are trained to put aside books for her and welcome her with big smiles. It is as though she has built up a Book Spy Network.

When it comes to the main bookshop, many of the books I stock are hard to source. I rely on estates and people downsizing, I scour charity shops and the internet, and I work in with other book dealers, especially Brian from Vintage in Dunedin. I also have a couple of buyers who help. My best roving buyer, Rebecca, locates books for me all the time, and Vicky has joined my book searchers' team. Vicky and her partner Steve are always on the lookout for stock for their second-hand and antiques shop, also located here in Manapōuri.

When I asked them to look for copies of *A Short History of Tractors in Ukrainian* they thought I wanted a tractor book, so they never found that one, but they turn up with all sorts of other treasures.

Even so, the quality of books I want is hard to find. I don't just stock anything and everything, as I am restricted by the number of books I can fit on the shelves — around 1250 in total across the bookshops. I once quipped to a lovely elderly woman who approached the counter with an armful of books,

'Sorry, you can't buy more than five. I have only a small stock of books, and if everyone bought this many, my shelves would be empty!'

She looked taken aback, then replied, 'Oh! You're right — how considerate of you! I'll put one back.'

I quickly clarified that I was joking and she laughed.

I don't think I'll use that line any more . . .

Hence my bookshelves can sometimes look rather empty.

CHAPTER 27

THE BOOKSELLER AT THE END OF THE WORLD

I was in love with books from the age of seven. Our entire family were readers and our parents encouraged us. I had a precious small library by my bed that included the early *Noddy* series by Enid Blyton, *Charlotte's Web* by E.B. White and some Golden Books. Nanny gave me *Little Women* and *Good Wives* by Louisa May Alcott for my eleventh birthday, and from then I was hooked on the classics. Books by C.S. Lewis, Charles Dickens, Mark Twain, Lewis Carroll and Charles Kingsley quickly filled the shelves. I still have many of my childhood books.

I never planned to become a bookseller but somehow it's a passion I've now had for almost half my life. Our first bookshop was run out of the same building as Fiordland Ecology Holidays, the business we started in 1995. It grew slowly as passengers who came on our tours asked where they could find copies of the books we had in our on-board library. Initially in the office I offered only a few titles, mainly books written by local authors, or covering the areas we were taking passengers to. As demand grew, so did the piles of books, and soon we had a bookshop, which I named 45 South and Below.

It opened in 1997, and when we sold the charter business in June 2010, I couldn't bring myself to get rid of the books. Every book had a story to tell. Our small home was already full of books so all the boxes went into storage. Unbeknown to me at the time, the books were to find a new home in the Two Wee Bookshops, which I opened years later.

I found I missed bookselling, and Lance, after six years of being told this repeatedly, suggested I open another bookshop. And so, at the age of 71, I had a small bookshop built on our property by André Bekhuis from Ōtautau. André was full of ideas and turned out to have a shed full of treasures, including beautiful old windows. The bookshop had to be small enough that it did not need a building permit (i.e. under 10 square metres), it had to look old and inviting, and it needed strong bookshelves that could hold at least 700 books. This was going to be my retirement 'hobby'.

André built the first shop around the two beautiful half-circle windows and an old rimu door. From the outside it looks like a gypsy caravan; people stop all the time just to take photos. It arrived on the back of a big trailer and was moved onto the piles with the help of a tractor. We painted it green, blue and turquoise, incorporated a blackboard by the door, sealed the wooden interior and hung our old ship's bell at the door. We were finally ready to unpack my boxes of books.

Staying with us at the time were Jonathan and Lisa from Wellington. We first met them when they came and stayed in our wee garden hut as B&B guests and have been close friends ever since. Lisa works in a library and reads a book a week, as well as writing book reviews. Jonathan is a doctor who specialises in palliative care.

With great enthusiasm, Jonathan offered to help me unpack the boxes, clean and price the books and put them on the waiting shelves. This should have taken a few hours but Jonathan wanted to look at every book. If it had pictures, his progress slowed to a snail's pace. It was a day I will always remember and treasure, the stacking of the shelves.

The Wee Bookshop was ready to open.

From day one the brass bell rang often. More and more cars were stopping and people just appeared from nowhere, drawn to the Wee Bookshop by its colourful cuteness. I had to build a bike stand, and put chairs out the front so people had somewhere to sit while they waited to come in. I had expected only a few customers but it was a hive of activity. My new shop quickly had a life of its own and my 'hobby' was out of control!

If I'm out in the garden or inside the house I can hear the bell so I go and open up. This system works well during the quiet times but generally I am in the Wee Bookshop most of the day.

When five customers are in the shop it's a crowd and I find myself sitting outside to make more room. I quickly discovered that the small children's books section was extremely popular and there was not enough room for children to sit or lie outstretched on the floor reading, as they do. Something had to be done.

'I need about two metres more bookshelf space for the children's section,' I informed long-suffering Lance. This soon developed to: 'I think I need another bookshop totally dedicated to children.'

'I thought you said you only needed more shelf space?' he said. Then, 'I knew this would happen. Two bookshops? In Manapōuri? Ruth, this is not a hobby, it's a business. We're meant to be retired!'

Lance had been practising the art of retirement since we sold the charter-boat business and was at the point of perfecting it. I, on the other hand, was gathering speed.

So, off we went, back to see André the wonderful builder. He had a small cottage already built in his workshop that was perfect; all it needed was bookshelves. It arrived in October 2019, once again on the back of a big trailer, together with three men and this time with a huge crane to swing it over the existing bookshop onto the selected site flush with the fence.

We painted it orange, yellow, blue and green, with the door a bright red. I planted a small flower garden, hung bells and wind chimes along the front, stacked the shelves full of books, and the Children's Bookshop was ready.

The second Wee Bookshop was an instant success, not only with children but also with adults. We have to remember to warn the adults as they go in because the door is built for children. 'Duck your head as you go in,' we're always saying. Nevertheless, it's fairly common to hear a soft ring of the bell I have hanging above the door every now and then.

Susanna and Rhys arrived with their four children at the start of their Christmas holiday: Lulu and Mimi the twins and Jesse and Orenia. The family came to the Children's Bookshop every day, they loved books so much. They named the fluffy white sleepover cat Blizzard McMurray.

Months after the family left, a huge parcel arrived on my doorstep. They had sent me two incredibly beautiful fairy dolls, one blonde and the other brunette, sitting on individual swings. They are now part of the Children's Bookshop, seen frequently swinging outside under the small veranda in sunny weather.

Manapōuri now has around 230 permanent residents, only 1 per cent of the population of the Southland district. We're at the end of the road and miles from anywhere but we have Two Wee Bookshops — the smallest stand-alone second-hand bookshops in New Zealand. Sometimes we are a traffic hazard, with cars and campervans parked on both sides of our small street, as well as sometimes down our driveway or on the grass verge.

One day a niggling thought came to me: what if two Wee Bookshops weren't enough?

———

OVER THE LAST three years I have noticed that many men sit in their vehicles while their wives or partners come into the shop to browse. Women like to take their time going through the books, often in silence, but on occasion the shop is full of chatter and laughter. With their husband or partner sitting out in the car, many women feel under pressure to hurry. One man tooted his horn after a while; others just passive-aggressively start the car, or hover on the doorstep asking, 'Ready to leave yet?' 'Found a book you like yet?' 'I'm still waiting for you.' You should never rush a book purchase.

One day a farmer arrived dressed in his farm clothes and smelling like sheep. He was very polite and said he wouldn't come into the shop that day as I had other customers. 'I'll come back another day,' he said.

'No, just come in; we don't mind,' I said.

'Nah, been drenching and smell a bit ripe. See you next time, Ruth.'

After this kind of situation had played out a few times I decided I needed a third bookshop: an open-air, farmer-friendly shop specifically for men.

My market research — which was entirely made up of me asking customers what they thought of the idea — showed that men would really enjoy having a space to themselves.

'Love, I think I need another bookshop,' I broke the news to Lance after months of careful thought.

A sigh. 'Oh God, will you ever stop? Why another one?'

'One for men. Hunting, fishing, farming, tractors, trains and somewhere for them to sit.'

'And where will it go?'

'Right beside the Children's Bookshop, tucked into the fence.'

Lance grumbled. 'How are you going to look after three shops? You are already racing from one to the other and you're always saying you don't have enough books.'

'I will be the CBD of Manapōuri,' I declared. 'Men will have a reason to get out of their cars; they can sit on the seat and browse through the books. I'll put maps in one of the drawers . . .'

'And old *Playboys* in another drawer,' Lance laughed.

Lance had always encouraged my Wee Bookshops venture because he understands how much I love books and the importance of social interaction for me. Every morning he's with me when I open up, fixing whatever needs fixing — and something always needs fixing — and then bringing me cups of coffee and fruit smoothies throughout the day. When I'm busy he helps out in the shop. When the shops are *too* busy, I send customers next door into our home where Lance entertains them and makes them a hot drink while they wait.

When it came to my idea for a third bookshop he tried to stop me, as he didn't have a clear vision of what I was trying to achieve. But as my mind was made up, he finally accepted that it was going to happen.

I bought an old linen closet and employed another local builder, Ryan Kincaid, and soon a little hut started to take shape. During its construction all of my customers were very interested in the concept of a bookshop for men. 'Now you'll have *three* Wee Bookshops!' But I was determined it would have its own name and asked for suggestions. Well, there were plenty! Hole in the Wall, The Man's Closet, The Lad's Lair, Blokes' Books, ManGrove, The Sharing Shed, The Boy's Place, Man's Hole (!), Pent House, The Nook, The Outpost, The Book Shed, Men's Quarters and The Book Chest.

When Sue suggested The Snug I knew it was the name I was looking for.

The 'snug' dates back to Ireland in the late nineteenth century. It was, and in some cases still is, a small private room in a public house that is closed off from the main clientele. You paid a higher price for your beer in the snug. When my sister Jill and I were in Belfast we went to The Crown Liquor Saloon, one of the oldest pubs in Northern Ireland. It had little booths with doors that you closed for privacy, and when you wanted service you rang a bell.

My Snug is a small, relatively private place. It has a covered veranda with a built-in bench seat. Growing over it is a beautiful lacebark tree, a hoheria, that is covered with tiny white flowers in spring. It has been suggested by some of the farmers that I serve wine or beer, but I can't as I don't have a liquor licence (thank goodness).

On the day I opened, one of my dear regulars, Terry O'Toole, arrived with his wife, Faye. They were both born in Bluff, I would say about 65 years ago. Terry is a great storyteller, his renditions involving a lot of shouting, face-pulling and enthusiastic gesticulation. As there were a few customers around when they arrived, Terry went back to his car to get his push-button accordion. Much to everyone's delight, he stood under the veranda of The Snug and started to play all the old songs. It was a perfect setting and a perfect opening for The Snug, the third instalment of my tiny bookshops.

TALES FROM THE BOOKSHOPS: A BOOKLOVERS' COMMUNITY

TWO WOMEN ON holiday came in one day and introduced themselves as Irene and Sue. They had met when they were in their thirties and have had a bond ever since. Irene now lives in a retirement village and comes to Manapōuri with Sue and her husband Tony for weekends and holidays. They love Manapōuri; when they come over from Blackmount and drop into the Fiordland basin, Sue says it's like coming into a whole different world.

A couple of days before Christmas I found they had left a tin of homemade ginger biscuits on my doorstep with a note thanking me for my time and the books I had recommended. When I next saw them I returned the biscuit tin. The ginger biscuits had been so delicious I asked if she would refill the tin in exchange for another book.

'Oh, I couldn't do that!' Sue said. Sue is a giver, and finds receiving gifts difficult.

A few weeks later Sue turned up with a bigger tin of biscuits. She handed me the tin with a cheeky smile. 'Take a book, Sue,'

I said. She shook her head. 'No, but I'll buy one.'

About a month later when I came home from Te Anau, there, hanging on my front door was a black supermarket bag. Eagerly looking inside, I found a biscuit tin full of hokey-pokey biscuits, another gift from Sue.

A few weeks later Sue and Irene came back to the bookshop. I returned the supermarket bag and the tin and requested more biscuits. This time I was determined to give Sue a book in return for her incredible kindness and eventually, after some encouragement from Irene, I succeeded. Sue relented and took *Fiordland* by Peter Beadle.

She had gone to primary school with Peter Beadle's son Simon. Peter Beadle was one of New Zealand's leading landscape artists. He died in February 2021.

Sue is a romantic at heart. One of her favourite authors is Jude Deveraux, author of over 40 historical romances.

I asked Sue if I could write about her in my book and she agreed. It was on her fifty-ninth birthday that we sat down to talk about what I would write. She sent me a note afterwards:

> *To Ruth. Thank you for the wonderful gift of*
> *including me in your book. It's a lovely 'Birthday*
> *Present' and one I will always treasure. Sue xx*

I felt like crying. Here was this beautiful lady thanking me for writing about her. Shouldn't it have been the other way around? She went on:

You have to be content and happy to bake.
My mother was a baker and I watched her
make pressed biscuits filled with jam and also
shortbread. My husband loved ginger biscuits
so I decided to make him some; he didn't believe
I could make them as good as the bought ones.
All of the family get biscuits made with love at
Christmas time. To Ruth they are yummy and
crispy and to see her face light up is a precious
gift in itself. Why not treat her to more?

It was Sue who came up with the name for my third bookshop, The Snug. Through my Wee Bookshops I have gained a wonderful friend who makes the yummiest ginger biscuits, but, like so many famous chefs, she will not give me the recipe!

CHAPTER 28

HOME STREET

O n 28 February 2020 the first case of Covid-19 was reported in New Zealand. When the country's borders closed on 19 March, I closed my bookshops. On 25 March our entire nation went into self-isolation and a state of national emergency was declared.

During the next six weeks I cleaned my entire stock of books, the shelves and even the cash. Once a week Lance and I drove the 20 kilometres to Te Anau to collect our weekly groceries.

Over the few years I have been operating, a rural women's book group has developed in our area. I try to read a couple of books a week, usually at 3.30 a.m. when

I can't sleep, so I can confidently recommend books to my customers. When I come across a really good one I take it to Alva or Shirley, or Sarah comes and picks it up. From there it goes to Catherine and Iona, then Margaret and Fi, occasionally to Edith and other women who live around the Te Anau and Manapōuri basin. When the book returns to the bookshop it is then sold, unless I want to keep it for my own bookshelves.

On grocery days during the 2020 lockdown I dropped off cleaned books to some of my regular customers and members of the random reading group, leaving them in letterboxes or on doorsteps. *The Feather Thief: Beauty, obsession, and the natural history heist of the century* by Kirk Wallace Johnson, *The Unlikely Pilgrimage of Harold Fry* by Rachel Joyce, and *The Language of Flowers* by Vanessa Diffenbaugh were among the favourites.

On 13 May we went down to Level 2 and, after seeking advice from the government-run Covid-19 business website, I reopened the main bookshop (on fine days). As the shops are so small, I could not let customers inside, so all trading took place outside. The books were on tables placed 2 metres apart, and on the front table was a bottle of hand sanitiser, a signing-in form and a notice asking people to stick to the Covid protocols — social distancing and so on. I asked customers to put aside any books they touched but did not buy. I then cleaned those books before I put them back on the tables.

Running a small shop in accordance with the guide-lines was difficult, but it was wonderful to see everyone after so long.

May is when it starts to get cold in Manapōuri. Conden-sation started appearing on the books on the outside tables and I had to continually dry them off. I usually close just after Easter for the winter, but 2020 was different because of Covid. I wanted to keep going as long as possible because it was like a little community centre, with everyone chatting and talking about how they had coped (or struggled to cope) during lockdown. Reading had been hugely important to many of them. My Two Wee Bookshops played a small but important part in the Covid story.

In the year since, possibly in response to the lockdowns, a number of small bookshops have opened across New Zealand. In Wānaka Jenny and Sally opened The Next Chapter, which already has a great reputation and we regularly send each other customers. It's as though people have rediscovered reading and the value of having books in your life. I had thought that when I reopened in September after lockdown my turnover would be down because of Covid. With our borders closed, my only customers would be Kiwis discovering their own country instead of going overseas, and of course my regulars.

But incredibly, trade that year was better than ever. Many of my customers were from up north and had never been to Fiordland or Stewart Island. They were astounded at the beauty; in awe of the wilderness and mountain landscape. Then they would drive past my Wee Bookshops.

'We just had to turn around and come back.'

'We've heard about you and your bookshops — just had to come and visit.'

'I heard you on Kim Hill's programme and wanted to meet you. Hope you've started writing your book!'

Yes, I had started my book. I couldn't say no to Jenny from Allen & Unwin, who convinced me my book would sell. Deep down I still wonder about that — but you're reading it, so thank you!

———

I BUILT THE third bookshop, The Snug, initially for men, but there are just as many women interested in farming, tractors, fishing and hunting. I have always been concerned that my books are mainly read by women, when I always wanted to reach out to men as well. There have always been good men in my life, who far outnumber the few who have bruised me and left scars. In many ways the scars I carry have, like weevils nibbling away on mash, given birth to something incredible.

Towards the end of writing this book, I went with Lance up to visit Joshua's cross. The beech tree is now over 20 metres high and Joshua's cross looks tiny and safe, tucked away under the strong lower branches.

We had friends with us so we wandered around the cemetery, Lance recalling the cowboy days of deer culling in helicopters when so many young men were killed, many of whom lie in that cemetery. A new section has been opened and a large sign lists the names of everyone buried there. On the opposite side is a map of the graves, each numbered, with the numbers cross-referenced to the names. I was studying this when there, away from everything else, I saw a small gold box on the map with the name JOSHUA inside it. I stared and stared, not believing what I was seeing: that he had at last been incorporated into the cemetery register.

'Lance! Lance!' I called. 'Come and look — Joshua is on the sign.'

All the other graves were numbered, but there, standing bravely to one side, was the name of my second son, Joshua. His was the only name on the map, a sure sign that his memory remains and that we have both made this home together, here in this small and beautiful part of New Zealand, at the end of the world.

I have always enjoyed the fact that to find the Two Wee Bookshops in Manapōuri you have to look for Home Street. It can take a very long time to find your home, but if you're lucky, you get there eventually. I did.

———

MY FATHER WAS right, my life has never been straight-forward and normal. So many of my friends tell me nothing surprises them when I come up with some anecdote from the past. As for Lance, he frequently tells everyone, 'Life is never boring when you are with Ruth.'

I was 38 years old when Andrew, my first son, became part of my life. Joshua's journey had come to an end, I was home back in New Zealand near my family and I was in love with an incredible man. Life had not passed me by; I had lived every minute.

Was I scarred — and scared? Many times.

Do I regret anything? No. All the events have shaped who I am today: determined, focused, hard to live with, deeply emotional, loyal and not easy to love.

I had a very dear uncle who loved me unconditionally. Whenever I went to see him he would smile, and say, 'Jesus Christ, what are you doing here, Ruthie? What the hell are you up to now?'

Now it is Lance and my close friends who accept me unconditionally. When they ask, 'What have you been up to? Who are you upsetting now?' I know that whatever my answer is, they will still love me.

I always believed that at some stage my life would 'level out', that I would throw out two anchors and achieve the socially acceptable status of 'normality'. In some ways I have, but even at the age of 75 I still have a rebel within, and for that I am thankful.

ACKNOWLEDGEMENTS

To Mike White, journalist, author and friend: without your encouragement, support and advice, this book would not have been written. Acknowledging you on this page cannot convey how grateful I am.

To Emma Clifton, my support angel: throughout the writing of this book, you put up with my tears, my doubts and my ramblings, and you always believed in my ability to tell my story. Our friendship grew over a year of frequent Zoom sessions. (I even watched Emma's wedding on Zoom!)

To Jenny Hellen, my publisher and one of the most positive people I know: how could I say no to you after our first Skype meeting? You kept me grounded and on track, and you walked with me all the way . . . not an easy task.

Thanks also to the wider team at Allen & Unwin, and to the editorial team: senior editor Leanne McGregor, copy editor Rachel Scott and freelance proofreaders Mike Wagg and Tessa King. Without your amazing skills my readers would have been in a state of total confusion!

To designer Saskia Nicol and illustrator Sophie Watson: thank you for the gorgeous design, especially the cover and endpapers.

To Marek, if you ever read this book: I have survived, and I hope you have also.

To Matt — you know who I mean — I sincerely hope you have found happiness.

To Tony: through this book, we have put the past behind us. Thank you for being so honest.

To Lance, my incredible husband: you have always supported me. You are my soulmate, my best friend, and the voice of reason when I am inclined to go astray. Thank you for your understanding and your love.

This book is also for our sons, Dane and Andrew, and our grandchildren, Isaac and Molly, Hina, Liam, Stella and Chloe. For you I have told my story. To my sister, Jill: you are so different from me, yet our love for each other is precious. Your two sons, Hamish and Keir — my nephews — will know now just how unusual their aunty is.

Without my friends who accept me as I am, I would not have had the courage to write this book. I cannot name you all, but I will thank you in person for being there for me and not judging me.

In the book's narrative, I have changed several names (and some circumstances) to retain the anonymity of the people involved. If I have made any mistakes, I am sorry: they are entirely mine.

ABOUT THE AUTHOR

Ruth Shaw runs a cluster of wee bookshops in remote Manapōuri in the far south of New Zealand. She lives on-site with her husband, Lance.